The # DIAPER DIARIES

THE REAL POOP ON A NEW MOM'S FIRST YEAR

by CYNTHIA L. COPELAND

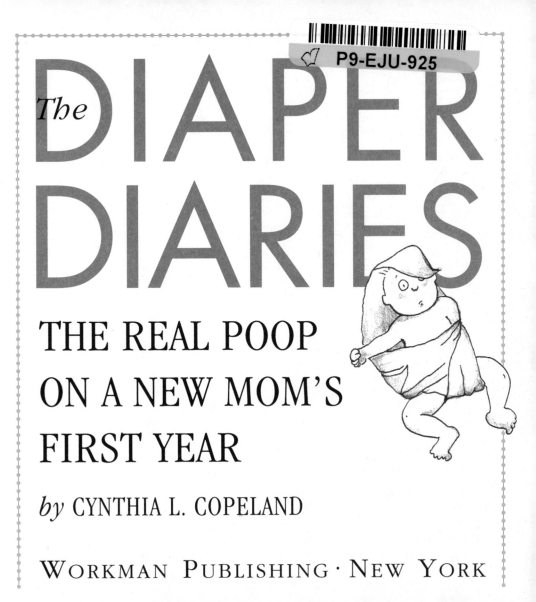

WORKMAN PUBLISHING · NEW YORK

DESIGN BY PAUL HANSON

LIBRARY OF CONGRESS CATALOGING-IN-PUBLICATION DATA
COPELAND, CYNTHIA L.
DIAPER DIARIES: THE REAL POOP ON A NEW MOM'S FIRST YEAR /
BY CYNTHIA L. COPELAND.
P.CM.
ISBN 0-7611-2860-3 (ALK. PAPER)
1. MOTHERHOOD—ANECDOTES. 2. MOTHERS—ANECDOTES.
3. BABIES—HUMOR. 4. PARENTING—HUMOR. I. TITLE.
HQ759.C74 2003
306.874'3--DC21   2003041062

WORKMAN BOOKS ARE AVAILABLE AT SPECIAL DISCOUNT
WHEN PURCHASED IN BULK FOR PREMIUMS AND SALES PROMOTIONS
AS WELL AS FOR FUND-RAISING OR EDUCATIONAL USE.
SPECIAL EDITIONS OR BOOK EXCERPTS ALSO CAN BE CREATED
TO SPECIFICATION. FOR DETAILS, CONTACT THE SPECIAL SALES DIRECTOR
AT THE ADDRESS BELOW.

WORKMAN PUBLISHING COMPANY, INC.
708 BROADWAY
NEW YORK, NY 10003-9555

WWW.WORKMAN.COM

PRINTED IN THE UNITED STATES OF AMERICA

FIRST PRINTING MARCH 2003
10 9 8 7 6 5 4 3 2 1

For Wayne,
my Number One guy

ACKNOWLEDGMENTS

Thank you to the warm and wonderful women who shared their new-mom moments with me. A special thanks to Jane, Becky, Lee, Julie, Mary, Helen, Kathy, Trish, Kristen, Cheri, Jenny, Cathy, Janet, Lisa, Deb, Lynn, Tonya, Lucy, Erin, Sandy, Carrie, Jeanine, Suzy, Martha, Paige, Laura, Samantha, Caroline, Sharlene, and Allyson.

Many thanks to the students at Fuller Elementary School who created new endings for classic lullabies.

Thanks also to my Workman friends: to Margot Herrera, my incredibly clever and always patient editor; to the delightful Liz Carey, for getting the project rolling; and to Paul Hanson, for appreciating my sense of humor and having such wonderful vision. It is a joy collaborating with the talented Workman folks.

CONTENTS

INTRODUCTION: LEARNING HOW TO MOM *vii*

IN THE HOSPITAL • *1*

OH BABY! • *39*

FEEDING AND WATERING • *75*

WASTE MANAGEMENT • *93*

THE NEW YOU • *105*

ZZZZZZZZZZZ • *121*

DOCTOR, DOCTOR • *139*

DAYS OF OUR LIVES • *151*

BABY MAKES THREE • *181*

OF GRANDPARENTS & GODPARENTS • *201*

NEW MOM SEEKS SAME • *217*

THE WEARING-TWO-HATS MOM • *239*

EPILOGUE: CONTEMPLATING THE FUTURE • *259*

his

hers

LEARNING HOW TO MOM

Congratulations! You made a new person! You get to name him, feed him, diaper him, force him to take piano lessons, make him "just taste it," and all of the other privileges of parenthood.

First, though, you need to learn how to mom. Before you had a baby, you may have thought you had all the answers. Now you realize you don't even know what most of the questions are.

Traditional books on parenting offer advice and information on everything from teething to lazy eye. They provide detailed instructions on taking an armpit temperature, explain the baby's rooting reflex, and describe how to clean your baby's teeth. Thank goodness for informative books like these because they keep pediatricians from being awakened at 3:35 A.M. to answer routine questions about colic and cradle cap.

But sometimes you need more practical information about your daily life as a new mom. You need to know how to make dinner with the five items you have left in your refrigerator or what your mother-in-law really means when she says, "You need to do things your own way, dear." You need to know that cute bibs stain but ugly ones don't. You need to understand baby math, as in: 1BI = 2BSO (One Bite In Equals Two Bites Spit Out).

And, even more important, you may need a reminder that laughter lightens the load. Despite the exhaustion, frustration, and sheer terror that accompany new parenthood, there are funny moments to be cherished and shared. If you can laugh today when your son pees on your just-dry-cleaned suit as you change his diaper, then you will be able to laugh three years from now when the same son pees in his pants during the Little Brick Preschool's performance of "The Farmer in the Dell." Humor is a habit.

Enjoy learning how to mom. It's a delightful process that lasts a lifetime. I wish you the best of luck.

IN THE HOSPITAL

Before you assume the position of 24-Hour-a-Day Mother, you have a brief 'tweener time in the hospital. I like to think of it as a minivacation courtesy of your health insurance provider, a little "thank you" for helping to keep the earth populated. Nice people will feed you, change your sheets, ask you how you are feeling, and teach you baby tricks like swaddling and burping. You're doing the mom thing, but you have major backup.

So much will transpire during your hospital stay. You will share news of the baby's arrival with friends and relatives, relaying vital information like the baby's weight, hair color, and name. The name you've chosen will elicit many comments, including which unappealing people share your baby's name ("the freakiest girl in my fifth-grade class was named Deirdre") and the multitude of ways it might be mispronounced or misspelled when your child enters school. You'll have a variety of visitors who will try hard to attribute the baby's cutest features to their favorite relatives of yours or your husband's. You will work to master the quick and easy diaper change, discover products like the Sore Nipples Solutions Kit (yes, really), and expand your vocabulary to include "latching on" and "fontanels."

After this crash course in new parenthood, you will return home where it seems your husband made a startlingly speedy return to his single-guy habits of using the treadmill as a clothes tree and seeing how high he can pile dirty dishes in the sink. But that, fellow moms, is fodder for a different chapter. . . .

A NEW STAR IS BORN

WITNESSES TO YOUR CHILDBIRTH EXPERIENCE

A Checklist

Birth is a sacred, intensely private act, right? Only those most intimately connected with you should be present. Well, if you're like most of us, as nice as that might sound, it's a far cry from reality.

Labor / Childbirth photos

Here is a list of all the people who are likely to have watched you give birth, based on a recently conducted national survey of new mothers.

Check all those that apply to *your* labor and delivery. Do not be concerned if you are not able to check every box. Chances are very good that anyone who did not witness this birth will catch your next one.

- [ ] THREE LABOR AND DELIVERY NURSES

- [ ] OB/GYN

- [ ] ANESTHESIOLOGIST

- [ ] FOUR MEDICAL STUDENTS

- [ ] HUSBAND

- [ ] MOTHER-IN-LAW

- [ ] BEST FRIEND

- [ ] BEST FRIEND'S COUSIN WHO IS VISITING FROM OUT OF TOWN

- [ ] VOLUNTEER FROM THE HOSPITAL GIFT SHOP

- [ ] FLORIST DELIVERY PERSON

- [ ] HOSPITAL CUSTODIAN

- [ ] GUY WHOSE WIFE IS IN LABOR TWO DOORS DOWN

- [ ] SOMEONE PASSING OUT MAGAZINES TO READ

- [ ] SIX-YEAR-OLD BOY WHO IS VISITING HIS NEW BABY SISTER

- [ ] EIGHT PEOPLE FROM A LAMAZE CLASS TOURING THE MATERNITY WING

- [ ] TEENAGE GIRL WHOSE MOTHER IS TRYING TO SCARE HER OUT OF HAVING SEX

NOMINEES FOR THE WORLD'S WORST LABOR COACH

So maybe your husband didn't rub your feet in the first stages of labor, or maybe he told you to say "hoo ha ha" instead of "hoo hoo ha" during the contractions. Maybe he flipped through the channels to try to get the score of the Red Sox game when he should have been getting you some ice chips. You may think that, as a labor coach, your guy wasn't exactly primo. But every bad has a worse, and here are a few of those.

After conducting a random survey of new mothers, my nominations for WORLD'S WORST LABOR COACH are:

RICK

"*On the day that I was to be induced for the birth of our first child, my husband didn't want to take a vacation day from work. So he lined up all these piles of paper all over my bed and started collating reports. He kept telling me not to move because I was shifting his piles.*" —SANDY

STEVE

"*My water broke while we were in bed, which my husband found repulsively fascinating. When we got to the hospital, he felt the need to repeatedly share exactly how much water there had been, saying that he was thinking he might have to go around town collecting two of every animal. He must have told that 'joke' 20 times.*"
—LIZ

VIC

"*I assumed that Vic, being a doctor, would be a great labor coach. Wrong! He came at the entire experience from an academic standpoint— on a clinical level, he was immensely interested but he seemed to forget that I was there. He spent the entire time chatting with the doctor and discussing in medical detail what was happening. I kept saying, 'Hey, Vic! Hello! Up here! Remember me?'*"
—KELLY

GREG

"*Greg got a new video camera three months before the baby was due. Instead of figuring out how to use it right away, he waited until I went into labor. He sat in a corner of the delivery room reading the instruction manual and had just figured out that the battery needed a day to charge before the first use as the doctor was holding Matthew up for us to see.*"

—MARYANNE

GARY

"*From centimeter one through nine during my labor with Chloe, Gary was sleeping in the labor bed while I was walking around trying to keep things moving. He even started snoring! The nurse brought* him *a blanket and a drink!*" —CARRIE

MY VOTE FOR
WORLD'S WORST LABOR COACH

☐ RICK
☐ STEVE
☐ VIC
☐ GREG

☐ GARY
☐ WRITE-IN
CANDIDATE:

....

THE CIRCUMCISION DECISION

Sure, you'll read up on the circumcision versus non-circumcision issue. You'll compare the statistics on kidney infections and STDs; you'll consider all of the potential surgical complications and future hygiene issues. Your husband will throw in his two cents, but it will all come down to this:

WHAT EVERYONE KNOWS 14-YEAR-OLD BOYS WANT TO HAVE IN COMMON WITH OTHER 14-YEAR-OLD BOYS:

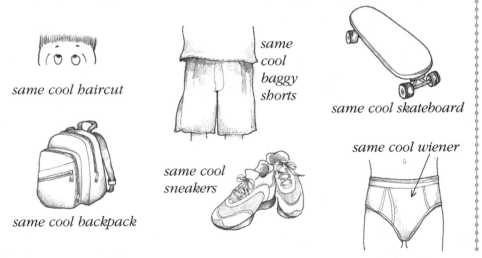

same cool haircut

same cool baggy shorts

same cool skateboard

same cool backpack

same cool sneakers

same cool wiener

PLACENTA POSSIBILITIES

As soon as the baby is born, you are faced with an important question: *What should you do with the placenta?*

There are a number of interesting possibilities. Take this revealing personality quiz to find out which placenta option is right for you.

What three items would you want to have with you on a deserted island?

a. *Binoculars, a bird-watchers' field guide, and a walking stick*

b. *Cell phone, pager, and Palm Pilot*

c. *My journal, ink, and a calligraphy pen*

d. *A keg, a good sound system, and a studly guy*

If you had only six months to live, how would you spend it?

a. *Meditating in the forest with my friends and lovers*

b. *Closing some major deals and shredding documents*

c. *Putting together a visual retrospective of my life*

d. *Getting all my buds together for a humongous party*

What was your most recent birthday wish?

    a. *To be as one with all the earth's creatures*

    b. *To be named CEO before I turn 30*

    c. *To make a meaningful statement with my creative work*

    d. *To be the Life of the Party, every minute, every party*

ANSWERS

If you answered A to most questions: Plant your placenta. Place the placenta in a hole in your garden, and plant a special bush or tree on top of it. Water regularly, and as the placenta breaks down, it will nourish your plant.

If you answered B to most questions: Sell your placenta. Sign documents authorizing the hospital to sell your placenta to a firm that will ship it overseas for use in manufacturing a variety of cosmetics. Demand 60 percent.

If you answered C to most questions: Make a placenta print. Lay the fresh placenta on a sheet of art paper to make a print. After it has dried, frame it and hang it over the sofa.

If you answered D to most questions: Have a placenta party! Invite your least squeamish friends over and serve up placenta pizza, placenta stew, and placenta lasagne.* To drink, blend the following ingredients into a placenta cocktail: $\frac{1}{4}$ cup raw placenta, 8 oz. V-8 juice, $\frac{1}{2}$ cup shredded carrots, and 2 ice cubes. Mmmm-mmm.

If you couldn't find yourself in the answers to any of these questions (who makes up these quizzes, anyway?), then your best option is to allow the hospital staff to dispose of your placenta.

*I'm not kidding! Recipes can be found on the Internet at www.geocities.com/virtualbirth/placenta.html *and* www.gentlebirth.org/archives/etplcnt2.html.

NAMING THE BABY

You would think that naming the baby would be an easy task compared to getting pregnant; suffering through nine months of leg cramps, backaches, and heartburn; and surviving childbirth. But no, these Naming Negotiations are trickier than anything that was ever hashed out at Camp David.

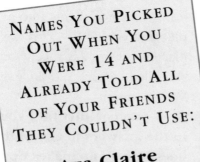

NAMES YOU PICKED OUT WHEN YOU WERE 14 AND ALREADY TOLD ALL OF YOUR FRIENDS THEY COULDN'T USE:

Ava Claire
Gabriel Trey

NAMES HE HEARD AT THE GYM TODAY AND KINDA LIKES BETTER THAN YOURS:

Tiffany
Buddy

How you compromise . . .

YOUR BACK-UP LIST (FOR A GIRL)	HIS BACK-UP LIST (FOR A GIRL)
Charlotte *(after Charlotte Brontë, author of* Jane Eyre*)*	**Alita** *(busty chick on the Latin soap opera he watches whenever he's home sick)*
Jacqueline *(as in the former First Lady)*	**Madonna** *(no explanation necessary)*
Brigit *(Celtic goddess of fertility, healing, and poetry)*	**Roxanne** *(from the Police song)*
Josephine *(after the Empress, wife of Napoleon)*	**Frieda** *(after his mother)*
Katherine *(of Aragon, your favorite of Henry VIII's six wives)*	**Katie** *(after his hottest prom date)*

YOUR BACK-UP LIST (FOR A BOY)	HIS BACK-UP LIST (FOR A BOY)

Donatien
(from the French, meaning "gift")

Bo
(as in Jackson)

William
*(as in Wordsworth,
the British poet)*

Clint
("Make my day...")

Erikson
*(after the King of Denmark in
the 12th century)*

Larry
(or Curly or Mo)

Frederick
*(like Frederick Grant Banting,
Nobel Prize, 1923)*

Slyk
(like the pro wrestler)

Harrison
(yes, as in Ford)

Fred
*(after Fred "yabba, dabba,
doo!" Flintstone)*

FINAL DECISION
*(after factoring in extra Mom points for suffering with
stretch marks and hemorrhoids)*

Katherine Claire and **Frederick Gabriel**

NAMES TO AVOID

Because the name you choose will have a significant impact on your child (determining, for instance, whether he spends recess chasing or being chased), strike these from your list of potential baby names:

Aine: Pronounced "on ya." Of course you are the only one who will know that. She will always dread the first day of school because she will have to tell the teacher how to say her name at least three times. When she's in middle school, she'll get to correct six or seven teachers on the first day.

Ashley: This name dooms your child to a last initial: Ashley M., Ashley H., etc. There are just too many darn Ashleys.

Britney: The Britneys of today will be the Esthers and Pearls of tomorrow.

Candy: Destined to be a stripper.

Cody: Like so many boys' names, it's cute through age five, then it's a burden.

Damian: Just go for broke and name him "Lucifer" or "Satan."

Donald: Duck.

Graham: The kid could be the next Stephen Hawking and all people will think of is the cracker.

Karen: Went out with Kathy, Jackie, Linda, Debbie, Barbara, and, dare I say it, Cindy.

Logan: Don't look to the soap stars for name ideas. As soon as Logan, Skylar, Trey, or Brody is shot by his ex-lover's stepson and is off the soap, the name will start its downhill slide toward uncool.

Simon: "Simple Simon met a pie man . . ."

Zach: He will be the last one to be Special Person of the Day, Line Leader, and Snack Person because he is a "Z." And there will be oh so many people who don't understand that it rhymes with "back," not "batch."

NICKNAMES

As soon as the baby's name becomes public, everyone will feel compelled to react, much like the judges at a figure skating competition. (Saying "I knew a strange boy in my Cub Scout troop with that name" is the equivalent of a 3.1.) Those friends and relatives who were miffed at being left out of the naming process will probably insist on bestowing a nickname.

Be Careful. A child's nickname can have a dramatic impact on his or her future. Consider the real-life cases illustrated opposite.

ADVICE FROM PEOPLE WITHOUT CHILDREN

"Just let the neighborhood kids give him a nickname."

WINTHROP TUCKER III

KATHERINE CLAIRE JONES

NICKNAME:
"WAMMER"

Hangs around parking lot of 7-11; has girl-friend named "Toots"; collects shot glasses and beer caps

NICKNAME:
"WIN"

Captain of high school tennis team; president of Chess Club; owns three blue blazers; run-ning for open seat on school board

NICKNAME:
"K.C."

Co-captain, field hockey team; president, Young Feminists of Loudon County; only girl on boys' lacrosse team; vegetarian

NICKNAME:
"KITTY"

Runner-up, Miss Teen Loudon County; cheer-leader since second grade; founding member and current V-P, Poodle Club of Springfield

PERFECTLY UNIQUE

When you were pregnant, you no doubt mentally explored all of the possible genetic combinations for your baby.

There were the best-case scenarios: your husband's perfect lips; Aunt Evelyn's long, dark eyelashes; your mother's thick, chestnut hair. And there were the worst-case scenarios: Uncle Ernie's crossed eyes, cousin Robert's bobo ears, your brother's mono-brow.

Well, here's the good news . . . and the bad news: Every baby looks like Mr. Magoo. It doesn't matter if the parents are both supermodels or are both trolls— all babies have the same pinched, splotchy, squishy look. (The mono-brow and bobo ears will eventually show up, but not until your child hits preschool and is surrounded by frank, talkative peers.)

Why newborn babies wear ID bands . . .

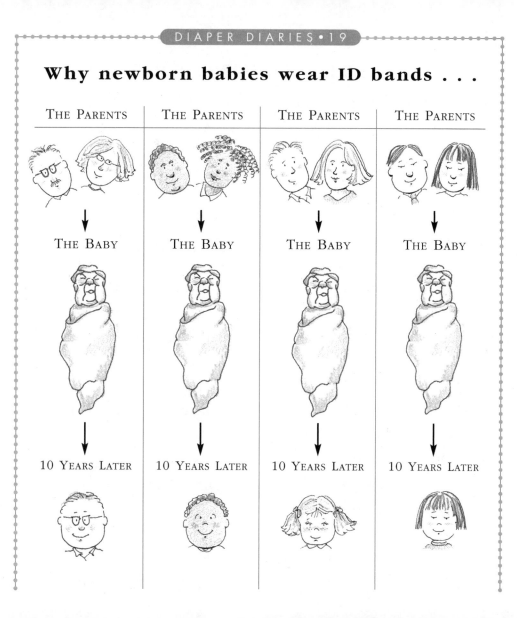

10 REASONS TO STAY IN THE HOSPITAL AS LONG AS YOU CAN

1. You can entertain visitors without having to cook, clean, or look nice.

2. The people who can't visit you send you flowers and nice gifts.

3. You get to eat every meal in bed, and when you're done, someone comes and takes the dirty dishes away.

4. You can nap whenever you want to.

5. Whenever you need anything, you just press a little button.

6. You can catch up on all of the soaps.

7. Everyone always wants to know how you're feeling.

8. You have a roommate, which is kind of like college all over again, but without the term papers.

9. When the magnitude of motherhood overwhelms you, you can send the baby to the nursery for a little while.

10. You can ask the nurses to feed the baby for you in the middle of the night.

5 THINGS YOU CAN SAY TO EXTEND YOUR HOSPITAL STAY

1. *"I haven't had a bowel movement yet and I don't think I'll be able to for a few more days—could even be a week."*

2. *"I'm just no good at this diapering thing. Can't I just prop him up on the toilet?"*

3. *"I'm so tired I think I might drop her."*

4. *"Oh! This isn't* my *baby I'm feeding? Jeez, they all look alike, don't they?"*

5. *"Can you help me look up 'Wet Nurse' in the Yellow Pages?"*

A NOCTURNAL ENVIRONMENT

There *are* a couple of drawbacks to being in the hospital, one of which is that most of the activity on the maternity ward seems to take place between 11 P.M. and 4:30 A.M.

Here's a typical nighttime schedule:

11:15 P.M. You drift off to sleep with the baby beside you.

11:52 P.M. A cheerful nurse bustles in to take your temperature.

12:23 A.M. Another cheerful nurse bustles in to take your baby's temperature.

1:04 A.M. The custodian vacuums (very thoroughly) and whistles ("Singin' in the Rain") in the hallway outside your room.

2:16 A.M. A lady from food services comes in to clear away your dinner tray.

3:42 A.M. The original cheerful nurse returns to check your sanitary pad* and take your blood pressure.

4:15 A.M. The 12:23 A.M. nurse returns to wake you up and ask if you want her to feed your baby so that you can sleep.

7:35 A.M. You awaken, and all is quiet on the maternity ward.

*It is this duty that led directly to the current shortage of nurses.

A TIME TO DWELL,
AND A TIME TO FRET

The other downside of being in the hospital is that you have the time to contemplate things that, once you are home, you will fortunately be too busy and exhausted to think about. Relax. Most of the worrisome things you are obsessing about right now will never happen. Some will, but the vast majority won't. Read on to put to rest some common fears.

6 THINGS YOU ARE WORRYING ABOUT RIGHT NOW THAT WILL NEVER HAPPEN

1. I will put the baby down somewhere and forget where I put her.

No, the good news here is that babies are always crying, so it is impossible to lose them.

2. I will drop something very, very heavy, like an anvil, directly on top of the baby's soft spot.

You will not do that. The baby's three-year-old cousin will do that, *but the baby will be absolutely fine. Babies are amazingly hardy little creatures.*

3. I will suck the baby's brain out through the nasal bulb syringe thingamajig.

In this case, I'm not sure your concern is completely unfounded. I would recommend trying to avoid the nasal bulb syringe thingamajig altogether.

4. The lovely name that we have so carefully selected for our child will become linked with an infamous person, like Monica.

Very unlikely. Think of the millions of nice names out there relative to the small number of infamous people. A much more likely scenario is that your teenage daughter will decide that she would prefer the name of an *infamous person to her given name, and will make it legal when she turns 18.*

5. The baby's umbilical stump will fall off while she's napping and she'll swallow it.

No, no. She won't swallow her umbilical stump. But by the time she is a two-year-old, she will *have swallowed a paper clip, a Lego block, some leftover cat food, the knob from a radio, one of your earrings, and a Barbie shoe.*

6. I will fail to introduce a second language at the optimum time, and my child—who would have grown up to be the head of the United Nations—will instead become a serial killer.

Worry not: Babies are not lumps of clay to be molded by their parents. They arrive with their own agendas. If he's meant to be a serial killer, your language tapes will have absolutely no impact on his destiny.

MATCH THE SWADDLE WITH THE SWADDLER

Swaddling a baby is like trying to line up all the colors on a Rubik's Cube. Once you know how it's done, you can do it over and over. But until you've figured it out, you're utterly confused.

Nurses have had lots of practice: year after year of dozens of daily swaddlings. New parents, however, have to prioritize, with feeding and diapering ahead of swaddling on the Must-Master List. But we all make a valiant effort, even if the results are a tad pathetic.

Can you match the Swaddle with the Swaddler?

ANSWERS: *a:* New Dad (the "wrap-her-up-like-a-half-eaten-hoagie" method). *b:* Maternity Nurse; *c:* New Mom (the "baby-as-delicate-as-glass-figurine" method).

MATCH THE SWADDLE WITH THE SWADDLER

a.

b.

c.

Maternity Nurse

New Mom

New Dad

THE NOT-SO-SIMPLE ART OF BREAST-FEEDING

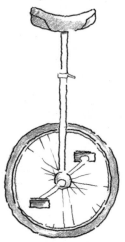

Like the Michael Jackson moon walk, nursing a baby is trickier than it looks. That's why there are people whose sole job it is to teach you how to do it . . . and why there is a whole industry built around breast-feeding paraphernalia: pumps, pads, pillows, etc. (And you thought all you needed were two breasts . . . silly you.)

ADVICE FROM PEOPLE WITHOUT CHILDREN

"It should come naturally, with that whatdayacall 'maternal instinct.' I mean, the cave women managed to breast-feed without lactation consultants, right?"

10 THINGS THAT ARE AS DIFFICULT TO MASTER AS NURSING

1. Riding a unicycle

2. Driving a delivery truck through the streets of Manhattan

3. Learning to write with Chinese characters

4. Understanding why $E=MC^2$

5. Grasping the concept behind Pokémon and Yu-gi-oh!

6. Making a decent hollandaise sauce

7. Explaining the difference between a porpoise and a dolphin

8. Knowing when to use "farther" and when to use "further"

9. Swimming the butterfly stroke

10. Drawing a picture of a galloping horse

BREAST-FEEDING REALITIES

There can be some minor discomfort.

Suffocation is a real possibility.

The baby may become attached to a particular breast.

The "latch-off" technique is at least as important to master as the "latch-on" technique.

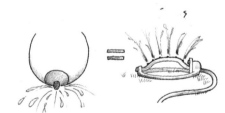

Your nipple is a lot more like a lawn sprinkler than the nipples that come with the baby bottles.

SPREADING THE NEWS

Used to be new parents bought a packet of Hallmark birth announcements, filled in each one with the pertinent info, and mailed them out. Today's parents, however, have a plethora of announcement options.

Many parents want to get the word out in a unique and clever way. Perhaps this is because with today's technology, everyone already knew the baby's height, weight, gender, IQ, and favorite color before she was even born. But in your attempts to be creative, you may fall prey to the Bordering-on-Ridiculous-Birth-Announcement Syndrome. Try to avoid the "punny" approach, like those announcements that play off the names of candy bars. Announcements in haiku or limerick are probably not good choices either.

Perhaps the most common birth-announcement faux pas parents make these days are Too Much Information and Uneventful Event. You'll want to avoid both ends of the birth-announcement spectrum:

THE "UNEVENTFUL EVENT" SYNDROME

This message is not flagged. [Flag Message - Mark as Unread]

Date: Fri, 13 Dec 2002 10:02:54 -0800 (PST)

From: "Williams, Marcy" | mwill@corporation.com

Subject: FYI

Attn: Customer Service, Accounts Receivable,
Sales and Marketing

       Please take note of the following:
- There have been numerous complaints about people taking lunches that do not belong to them from the staff refrigerator. Eleanor's lunches seem to be especially popular. Please, if the bag says "Eleanor" on it, and that is not your name, do not take it.
- I apologize for any inconvenience my absence last week may have caused. I delivered a baby on Wednesday (girl, 7 lbs., 8 oz., healthy) and was out of the office for the remainder of the week. A list of rescheduled meetings is posted on my door.
- Today's training session on how to operate the new photocopier has been postponed. The trainer was called away on an emergency.

       Thank you for your attention to these matters.
    —Marcy

Do you Boohoo!?
http:/www.diapercorporation.com

THE "TOO MUCH INFORMATION" SYNDROME

JEANINE AND DOUGLAS WELL[...]
JOYFULLY ANNOUNCE THE BIRTH OF THEIR DAUGHTER!

Laura Elizabeth Wells

WAS BORN ON MARCH 12 AT 4:37 P.M.
AT HOLY CROSS HOSPITAL IN SPRINGFIELD.
SHE WEIGHED 7 LBS., 2 OZ. AND WAS 21⅝" LONG.

HER APGAR SCORE WAS 9. SHE HAS HER FATHER'S LOVELY, THICK EYELASHES AND HER MOTHER'S DELICATE FINGERS. FOR MORE INFORMATION ABOUT LAURA, PLEASE CHECK HER WEB SITE AT **PERFECTLAURA.COM.**

JEANINE INITIALLY INTENDED TO HAVE AN UNDERWATER BIRTH, BUT AFTER 10 HOURS WITH NO SIGNIFICANT PROGRESS, SHE DECIDED TO ATTEMPT THE SQUATTING POSITION. THIS ALSO PROVED DIFFICULT AND, THREE HOURS LATER, SHE ELECTED TO MOVE TO THE LABOR BED AND HAVE AN EPIDURAL, WHICH DECREASED THE PAIN BUT ALLOWED HER TO CONTINUE TO FEEL THE CONTRACTIONS. THE BABY WAS DELIVERED WITHOUT INCIDENT, BUT JEANINE'S PERINEUM TORE, REQUIRING EIGHT STITCHES, WHICH WILL CAUSE SORENESS AND DISCOMFORT FOR SEVERAL DAYS TO A WEEK. SHE ALSO EXPERIENCED SOME BRUISING AND BROKEN CAPILLARIES AND IS HAVING A GREAT DEAL OF DISCHARGE.

JEANINE'S MILK FINALLY CAME IN, THOUGH SHE IS HAVING SOME TROUBLE BREAST-FEEDING BECAUSE OF SORE, CRACKED NIPPLES. SHE IS ALSO SUFFERING WITH HEMORRHOIDS. OTHERWISE MOTHER AND BABY ARE DOING WELL.

MOMMY NEEDS HELP

There comes a time when you can no longer postpone the inevitable: You have to go home. No more comforting, omnipresent nurses; no more handy call button; no more eating lunch in bed while watching *I Dream of Jeannie* reruns.

Filling in this "Mommy's Weekly Helper" form will make your departure from the hospital much less traumatic. Your goal should be to have all of the blanks filled in before you return home. That way, you can be assured of having someone

Why would they allow this perfect baby to go home with ME? Don't they know I can't balance my checkbook? Never iron? Have cobwebs in my skylights? Lose my sunglasses at least once a week?...

there to help you with the baby until it is time to enroll him in preschool. (Don't overlook people from your past: former classmates, roommates, co-workers, neighbors. What better way to reconnect than over changing, feeding, and burping your baby?)

"Mommy's Weekly Helper"

WEEK 1: ....

WEEK 2: ....

WEEK 3: ....

WEEK 4: ....

WEEK 5 ....

WEEK 6: ....

WEEK 156: ....

WEEK 157: ....

WISHFUL THINKING

What you thought you'd look like leaving the hospital (based on Pampers commercials and skinny sitcom moms).

- Doting husband/proud father

- Perky hairdo

- 6-month-old baby (even though you only had her 3 days ago)

- Bag brimming with dozens of thoughtful and expensive gifts

- Size 6 hip-hugger jeans that you couldn't fit into even *before* you got pregnant

REALITY CHECK

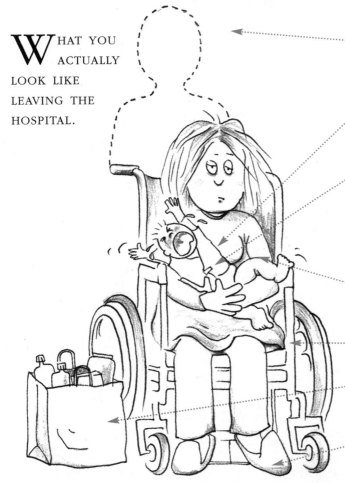

WHAT YOU ACTUALLY LOOK LIKE LEAVING THE HOSPITAL.

- *Husband went to talk with a guy from his bowling team who is there for an X ray*

- *Baby starts crying for the first time as you leave the hospital*

- *Baby is wearing hospital T-shirt and diaper because Baby Dior dress was too scratchy and complicated*

- *Maternity clothes you wore into the hospital*

- *Donut pillow for hemorrhoids*

- *Bag filled with stuff the hospital won't miss*

- *Husband's slippers because your feet are fatter, too*

OH BABY!

How hard can it be to take care of one little baby? He orders from a very limited menu, he pees and poops in a contained space, and when he's tired, he sleeps. What could be more simple? People have been successfully turning babies into toddlers for eons.

But it's not as easy as it seems. First of all, babies seem to require a lot of stuff. And their stuff is big. Big and plastic and brightly colored. (Interestingly, the older kids get, the smaller their stuff gets. By the time your son's 12, he'll just need 20 bucks, a baseball, and a Gameboy Advance. By the time your daughter's 12, she'll just need 20 bucks, glittery eye makeup, and a portable CD player. So you will get your living room back eventually.)

Second, babies don't behave the way you think they will. When they are tired, for instance, they don't act sleepy—they act very awake and cranky. It is up

to you to convince them that they are ready for a snooze. And if you miss the initial sleepy window, then you're into the Oxymoronic Zone of Overtired Yet Less Sleepy, which means it will be three times as hard to get them to take a nap.

And third, you just can't keep up with them. As soon as you adjust to your baby's napping schedule of a morning nap, an early afternoon nap, and a dinnertime doze, he's changed his game plan and you've got to reboot.

But babyhood is temporary. The days may seem long, but the years fly by. And when you are coping with the Glittery-Eye-Makeup-Portable-CD-Player phase, you will think back, misty-eyed, on the Up-Every-Two-Hours-but-You-Got-to-Pick-Her-Friends phase.

PARAPHERNALIA

Let's be honest. Most baby items are really for mommies. Baby swings? They keep the baby happily in motion while you go to the bathroom, make a phone call, and load the dishwasher. The beautiful cloth doll with the handmade clothes? That goes up on a shelf in the nursery; the baby drags around a bald troll she found at the park.

In truth, babies can do without a lot of the pricey paraphernalia we moms have deemed indispensable. Surely you've noticed that a baby will enjoy and appreciate an item in inverse proportion to the cost of said item. In other words, he'll spend about 27 seconds focused on the stand-alone computerized infant learning center ($199.99) and four hours happily whacking the coffee table with one of the pieces of Styrofoam packaging. So it makes sense to find free or inexpensive substitutions for many of the more expensive baby items.

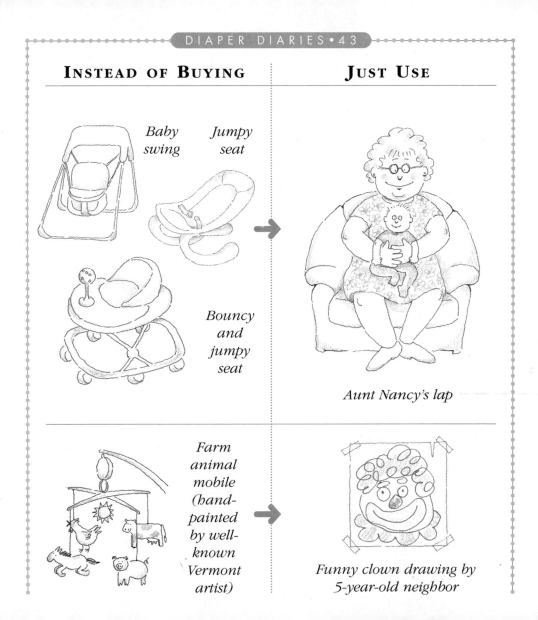

INSTEAD OF BUYING

JUST USE

Baby swing

Jumpy seat

Bouncy and jumpy seat

Aunt Nancy's lap

Farm animal mobile (hand-painted by well-known Vermont artist)

Funny clown drawing by 5-year-old neighbor

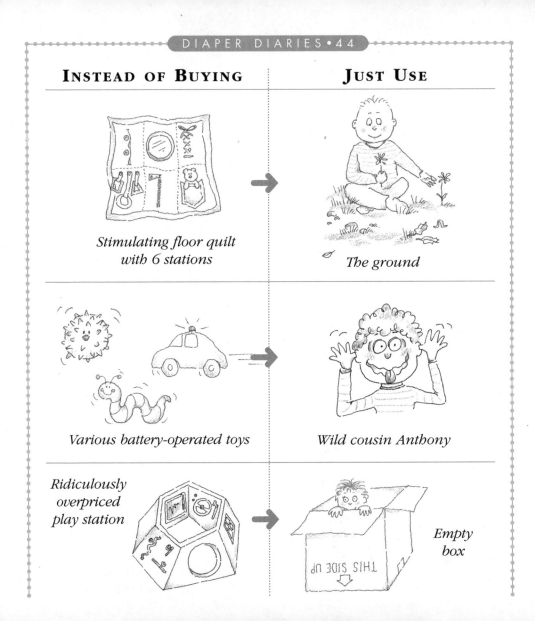

INSTEAD OF BUYING	JUST USE
Stimulating floor quilt with 6 stations	The ground
Various battery-operated toys	Wild cousin Anthony
Ridiculously overpriced play station	Empty box

INSTEAD OF BUYING	JUST USE
CDs designed to stimulate baby's interest in music (and indestructible CD player)	Daddy's songs (and indestructible Daddy)
Toys guaranteed to provide hours of enjoyment	Roll of toilet paper

LET'S TALLY UP OUR SAVINGS

Total cost of baby paraphernalia pictured here: **$1,045.20**

Total cost of suggested substitutes: **$36.77**

ITEMIZED:

- *Feeding Aunt Nancy lunch: $9.43*
- *Replacing items broken during wild cousin Anthony's visit: $24.50*
- *Toilet paper: $.69*
- *Earplugs for when Daddy sings: $2.15*

BABY STUFF

As we've seen, many seemingly indispensable baby items are anything but.

And yet there are lots of things you really need but never thought of getting (or inventing) until you were right smack dab in the middle of mothering. Here are a few:

Some sort of rearview mirror setup so that when the baby is in the backpack, you can see if she has spit up all over your hair or has inadvertently shoplifted a straw hat from Wal-Mart.

A three-foot-long grabber thingamajig like they have at the supermarket for those times when the baby falls asleep on you and you want to grab the TV remote or your novel, which is always just beyond your reach.

A periscope so that you can look around the corner into the nursery (without being seen) to determine if the baby is playing contentedly and quietly or slowly choking to death on her bootie pom-pom.

Something to pry open the baby's mouth when you suspect she's gumming something funky.

Ten pairs of booties that are exactly alike because you will lose one bootie in each pair over the course of the first two months.

A blanket that clings to the baby all night long to relieve you of nighttime re-cover duty.

A device that automatically responds to the baby's 3:17 A.M. cry by projecting an image of your face on the baby's wall and playing a recording of you saying soothing things.

A teeny tiny baby hammock that will keep the baby from rolling onto his tummy while he sleeps and will also keep him feeling snuggled.

TRUE STORIES

THE PACIFIER

"*When Lindsey was a baby, she was absolutely addicted to her pacifier, which she called her 'hup.' If she lost her hup in the middle of the night, she became hysterical and my husband and I would have to get up and conduct an all-out search.*

We decided that the smart thing to do would be to get her another pacifier. That way, even if she couldn't find one hup at night, she'd have a back-up. What we didn't anticipate was that she became addicted to both *hups: She had her regular mouth hup, and now she had her hand hup. We thought about getting a third one, but the way it was going, we figured it would end up being a toe hup.*"

—JULIE

LOVEYS

Loveys. Just one more category to add to your list of "Baby Ironies." As a sane and reasonable person, you assume that your baby will become attached to an item that has a measure of appeal, either from a visual or tactile perspective (like, it's cute or it's fuzzy). But babies aren't following the Sane and Reasonable Rule Book. In fact, the less cuddly and more mundane an item is, the more babies seem to like it.

Don't even try to figure this one out. Just go with it.

WHAT YOU BOUGHT WHILE YOU WERE PREGNANT FOR HER TO CUDDLE WITH

Chenille teddy bear ($74.99)

Hand-knit afghan (in stimulating patterns & colors)

Squishy doll (no chokeable parts) from FAO Schwarz

Fuzzy ball with tinkling bells inside

Soft doggy that plays four different lullabies

WHAT SHE *WANTS* TO CUDDLE WITH

TV remote

Spooky plastic doll's head

Cow candle

Your makeup brush

Whatever you bought at the store today

Ear from $74.99 chenille bear

The Phone Book

Flower lamp

Chicken potholder

TRUE STORIES

THE LOVEY

"*Thomas is very attached to this tacky, plastic doggy head rattle he got when he was just a few months old. He's always clutching it in his hand, even when he's asleep. Recently, we went on a trip and had Thomas with us in our hotel room. Every hour or two, my husband and I were awakened by this ferocious rattling noise. It seemed that Thomas would have an intense dream, which would make him shake the rattle. The noise would crescendo as he got to the climax of the dream, then gradually taper off as the dream ended. My husband plans to use his surgical skills to perform an 'operation' on the doggy and render him rattle-free.*"

—JUNE

ADVICE FROM PEOPLE WITHOUT CHILDREN

"*Oh, just throw that old blanket in the trash. By tomorrow, she'll have forgotten all about it.*"

"*My* daughter loves one of my black silk slips. She insists on dragging it with her everywhere: the grocery store, church, the park. It can be more than a little embarrassing."

—RACHEL

"*My* son will attach himself to anything that is bright orange . . . and I mean anything. For the entire month before Halloween, he is beside himself with glee."

—NAOMI

"*My* 10-month-old son Jeremy has a blue camel that he just adores. It is missing a leg, its tail caught on fire a few months ago, and it doesn't even remotely resemble its original color, but Jeremy won't go anywhere without it."

—JULIA

ENTERTAINING BABY

Much of your day involves thinking up new ways to amuse your baby. This can be a challenge. And you will realize early on that there are no residual effects of your valiant efforts to entertain. The minute your final peek-a-boo has come and gone, the baby goes right back to his original cranky mood. Sigh.

But you will have better luck if you play the games that your *baby* wants to play. (Chances are you'll end up playing those anyway.)

Babies aren't nearly as clever when you gather an audience.

GAMES BABIES WANT TO PLAY

MONTH **1**: You'll never guess when I'm going to spit up!

MONTH **2**: Let's see how long I can cry.

MONTH **3**: Where have I rolled to?

MONTH **4**: Who will pick up what I throw on the floor?

MONTH **5**: Guess what I just put in my mouth!

MONTH **6**: Which way will I tip when you sit me up?

MONTH **7**: I'll bite your nipple and you try not to jump.

MONTH **8**: What common household item will I be
afraid of today?

MONTH **9**: Bet I can reach what you think I can't!

MONTH **10**: Guess what strange Transitional Comfort
Object I'll be dragging around this week!

MONTH **11**: Lean over so I can grab your fingers
and stumble around!

MONTH **12**: Call me and I'll run and hide!

CRYBABY

HOW TO READ YOUR NEWBORN BABY'S MOODS

Babies have four basic moods or, shall we say, four variations on a single mood, which is fussy.

MOOD 1
CONTEMPLATING
REASONS TO CRY

MOOD 2
CRYING

MOOD 3
MOMENTARILY
DISTRACTED

MOOD 4
REVVING UP
TO CRY AGAIN

New babies cry all the time. Statistically, I believe the figure is 23.5 hours a day.

There is a general belief that a new mother can interpret what her baby's cry means, as in: This is a hungry cry; this is a diaper-needs-changing cry; this is a thread-wrapped-around-my-big-toe cry. Hogwash. Oh, you might be able to differentiate between a Fell-Out-of-My-Crib "Aaaaaaahhhhh" and a Bored-With-My-Life "Eh-eh-eh," but those are extremes. Don't believe me? See if you can correctly match *The Cry* with *The Meaning of the Cry* . . .

Keep things in perspective. It really won't last forever...

CAN YOU CORRECTLY MATCH THE CRY

CRY NO. 1	CRY NO. 2	CRY NO. 3

MEANING A	MEANING B	MEANING C
The baby is crying because she hates the "Princess and the Pea" decorating scheme you chose for the nursery.	The baby is crying because she has to eat strained beets while you are enjoying a bag of Doritos.	The baby is crying because she just wants to make lots of loud noise and this is her only option.

WITH THE MEANING OF THE CRY?

CRY NO. 4	CRY NO. 5	CRY NO. 6

MEANING D

The baby is crying because she hates it when you tape that pink bow onto her head. She feels it is humiliating, as the tape only draws attention to her baldness.

MEANING E

The baby is crying because she feels helpless and frustrated about global warming, the threat to the rain forests, and rising interest rates. (And she is upset about the way you voted in the last election.)

MEANING F

The baby is crying because you change her diaper too much. She likes warm and squishy wet diapers better than scratchy, dry new ones.

5 TRIED-AND-TRUE TIPS FOR TURNING OFF THE TEARS

Infants do four things very well: sleep, eat, make dirty diapers, and cry. They are especially good at crying. Unfortunately, their crying can be contagious. Before you decide to join in, try one of these funky methods to stop the tears:

"Sometimes you have to startle babies out of their tears. If Aaron is crying and I step outside, he immediately stops. I don't know if it's the temperature change, the breeze, the sunlight . . . something about being outside is distracting enough that he forgets he was unhappy."
—SANDY

"The 'airplane' works every time: I stretch the baby (on his tummy) along my forearm with his chin cupped in my hand and his legs straddling my

arm and then I 'zoom' him around the house. You just hope no one peeks in your window while you're doing this."

—LESLIE

"*Pouring water over the baby's head really works!* Wrap him in a receiving blanket, dim the lights, lower him into a warm bath, and pour cups of water over the back of his head until he calms down."

—NELL

"*Instead of rocking the baby from side to side*, hold him upright (supporting his head), and lift him up and down, up and down, repeatedly, until he stops fussing. (And in lieu of a gym workout, this is great for developing upper-body strength!)"

—DORI

"*Put the baby in a baby sling* and tap his butt in a repetitive pattern. This has worked for every one of mine."

—EILEEN

STAGES OF DEVELOPMENT

You may be familiar with the various stages of a baby's development during the first year. But how about *your* stages of development as a mother? You need to know how your developmental phases jibe (or don't) with your baby's.

FIRST MONTH

MOM: Develops ability to nap in 30-minute spurts to coincide with baby's schedule

BABY: Starts napping in 10-minute spurts

SECOND MONTH

MOM: Finally masters breast pump and is able to pump enough milk so Daddy can give the baby a bottle

BABY: Hates Daddy

THIRD MONTH

MOM: Has finally developed extensive repertoire of surefire ways to calm down very fussy baby

BABY: Stops being very fussy

FOURTH MONTH

MOM: Learns how to sleep without rolling over, thus eliminating fear of rolling on top of baby in "family bed"

BABY: Learns how to roll and is able to roll over any barrier set up on edge of "family bed"

FIFTH MONTH

MOM: Needs social interaction and joins play group

BABY: Shuns social interaction, deciding that other babies are merely competition for the world's toys, all of which are rightly his

SIXTH MONTH

MOM: Learns to let go of obsession with keeping house spotless

BABY: Learns to pick out and pick up tiny, inedible objects on floor several feet away, all of which must be tasted

SEVENTH MONTH

MOM: Ready to hire caregiver and return to work

BABY: Develops sudden and extreme fear of strangers

EIGHTH MONTH

MOM: Has become addicted to 2 A.M. reruns of *News Radio*

BABY: Finally starts sleeping through the night

NINTH MONTH

MOM: Focuses on creating homemade, organic meals for baby

BABY: Has developed taste for Burger King fries and Spaghetti-Os, presumably on Daddy's watch

TENTH MONTH

MOM: Has figured out how to put baby in backpack without help

BABY: Hates backpack because now he thinks he can walk (even though he really can't)

ELEVENTH MONTH

MOM: Finally adjusts to having baby clinging to her at all times, even when going to the bathroom

BABY: Suddenly has no interest in being anywhere near Mommy, especially in places like shopping malls and parking lots

TWELFTH MONTH

MOM: Is ready to begin weaning baby from breast

BABY: Knows where breasts are and how to get at them

TRUE STORIES

THE BABY MONITOR

"I couldn't live without a baby monitor, but it has gotten me into trouble. Once, when we had just moved into our new house, I put the receiver on the front porch so that I could do yard work while I listened for the baby to wake up from her nap. When I heard her cry, I went in to get her, but left the receiver with the volume turned up as high as it could go.

"A few hours later, I went into the baby's room to find that our dog, Haley, had pooped all over the new carpet. I was so annoyed that I immediately started yelling at the dog: 'Haley! You bad girl! Look what you did! I am just about ready to get rid of you for good! You are sleeping in the garage tonight. Do you hear me, Haley?!' None of our new neighbors knew that Haley was a dog and I'm sure they were more than a little anxious about having their children play at my house!"

—MARY

THINGS YOU CAN DO NOW
THAT YOU HAVE A BABY

There are plenty of things you can't do anymore now that you're a mom. You can no longer watch TV commercials for the Christian Children's Fund, for example. Not only are you a little suspicious of anyone who claims to be able to raise a child on 23 cents a day, but you are also heartbroken for all of those poor little darling babies.

But having a baby does allow you to do a *few* things that you couldn't do before:

Quickly end a phone call with your neighbor who sells life insurance

Pass gas and pass the blame

Be late everywhere

MILESTONES THAT MATTER

If you believe those fill-in-the-blank baby books, the important events in a child's life are things like the first smile, the first word, the first step. These are certainly highlights, but there are many other milestones in the first few years of a child's life that are of more practical importance to you as a mom.

Fill in the age at which your child reached the following truly Meaningful Milestones:

———— Straightens out the night/day thing just in time to prevent you from moving to the other side of the world so that you can get some sleep

———— Doesn't need to be in rear-facing car seat anymore so you no longer have to keep pulling the car over and checking to make sure he's still alive

———— Can grasp a toy, thus freeing you of the obligation of holding up toys for her to look at, or not holding up toys and feeling guilty about it

———— No longer shrieks from 5 P.M. to 7 P.M. every single night, which means that your husband will probably start coming home before 8 P.M.

_____ Stops throwing stuff off her high-chair tray just to see if you'll pick it up

_____ Is self-burping

_____ Figures out not to crawl under the coffee table and then try to stand up

_____ Can feed himself Cheerios out of a cup one at a time, which calculates to eight seconds of free time for Mom per Cheerio

_____ Moves out of the phase known as One-Nap-Is-Not-Enough-but-Give-Me-Two-Naps-and-I'm-Up-Until-11 P.M.

_____ Stops biting (okay, has stopped biting hard enough to leave marks) so you may rejoin your play group

_____ Can walk uphill and downhill, and not just on level ground, so you can now put her down outside without her tipping over

_____ Can locate errant pacifier in the middle of the night all by herself

_____ People outside the family actually understand what he is saying

_____ Is no longer afraid of balloons, which means you don't have to call ahead and ask for a description of the decorations before you attend a party

_____ Has a basic understanding of what items should not be flushed down the toilet

_____ Can blow her own nose

_____ Can sit on the regular toilet seat with relatively little chance of falling in

_____ Actually *comes* when you call him instead of turning it into a fun hiding game

_____ Provides more than 15 seconds' notice when he needs to go to the bathroom

_____ Can tell you what the babysitter was *really* like

_____ Realizes that picking his nose is gross and he should do it only when no one can see

_____ Is no longer afraid to sit on Santa's lap, though still believes in Santa (*Note:* This is a very short-lived phase, so enjoy it.)

_____ Can change Barbie's clothes without your help

_____ Knows whether or not the socks match the outfit

_____ Has figured out what it feels like just *before* throwing up

_____ Can go to a friend's house alone, so now she can be friends with kids whose moms you don't really like

_____ Is able to answer the phone and determine whether or not the person calling is a telemarketer

CRITICAL MILESTONE: WHEN YOUR CHILD CAN READ A NOTE

"*When it was time for me to deliver my second child (in the middle of the night, of course), I called my mother and asked her to come right over and stay with Jack, my three-year-old. As we prepared to leave for the hospital, my husband and I suddenly realized that Jack was going to wake up in the morning and come into our room as he always does— and no one would be there! He would be frantic! So my husband quickly drew big arrows on pieces of paper that we laid out on the floor leading from his room into the room where my mother was sleeping. It worked, but it certainly will be easier when he can read a note I've left for him!*"

—PATRICE

PROJECTING THE FUTURE

A new mom analyzes everything her baby does in an effort to envision what the future may hold. What character traits will evolve from her ability to suck both big toes at the same time or to transfer a teething ring from one hand to the other and back again? You're tempted to predict great accomplishments based on those early indications. But don't get overly excited, Mom: Just because your baby dribbles doesn't mean he's going to be the next Michael Jordan. (And, alternatively, just because he can put his foot in his mouth doesn't mean he's going to be the next Dan Quayle.)

Here's what I mean:

THE BABY TRAIT: The baby flails his arms.

YOUR PROJECTION: He will be a world-famous composer/conductor like John Williams.

MORE LIKELY: He will be one of the guys who waves planes into their gates.

THE BABY TRAIT: The baby likes to get her own way.

YOUR PROJECTION: Like Margaret Thatcher or Barbara Jordan, she will fight for her beliefs in the face of strong opposition.

MORE LIKELY: She will just be a bossy lady.

THE BABY TRAIT: The baby is not afraid of strangers.

YOUR PROJECTION: She will be the next Katie Couric or Barbara Walters, an engaging and popular television personality.

MORE LIKELY: She will be voted Best Wal-Mart Greeter by the other store employees.

THE BABY TRAIT: The baby shares his toys well at play group.

YOUR PROJECTION: He will be a politician like Franklin Roosevelt who fights for a more even distribution of the nation's wealth.

MORE LIKELY: He will be the guy in the neighborhood everyone borrows tools from.

THE BABY TRAIT: The baby is not afraid of getting his shots at the pediatrician's office.

YOUR PROJECTION: He will be like Dr. Jonas Salk, who developed the polio vaccine.

MORE LIKELY: He will be a tattoo artist in Atlantic City.

THE BABY TRAIT: The baby bangs his spoon on the high-chair tray.

YOUR PROJECTION: He will be a famous drummer like Buddy Rich.

MORE LIKELY: He will be the annoying guy in every meeting who gets bored and starts tapping his pencil on the table.

THE BABY TRAIT: The baby likes his plastic airplane toy best.

YOUR PROJECTION: He will be the pilot of *Air Force One*.

MORE LIKELY: He'll always volunteer to operate the kiddy airplane ride when the firefighters' carnival is in town.

THE BABY TRAIT: The baby loves watching videos.

YOUR PROJECTION: He will be a famous movie director or producer, like Steven Spielberg.

MORE LIKELY: He will be "Vic" at Blockbuster, as in "Vic's Picks."

FEEDING AND WATERING

Initially, feeding and watering the baby involves making a choice between the breast and the bottle (or concocting some combination of the two). Undoubtedly, you'll take many serious things into consideration: your health and the baby's, nutritional benefits, bonding issues, whether or not you plan to return to work within the first year . . . yadda yadda yadda.

But before you make your decision, have you mentally gone back to your childhood to assess your various talents and preferences? For instance, when you were a kid, did you like to make forts in the den out of two blankets, the recliner, and the coffee table and then hide there?

If so, you will find it a breeze to arrange scarves and shawls so that you can nurse discreetly in public. And think back on feeding your pets. If you always tried to get your sister to dole out the dog's kibble when it was your turn, you may prefer the anyone-can-take-your-place feature of bottle-feeding. No matter what objective information you are evaluating, a long-ago aptitude or inclination may be the decisive factor.

The choice is yours. The nice thing about this is that no matter what you decide, the baby will turn out just fine.

THE PRACTICAL CONSEQUENCES OF YOUR DECISION

Sure, there are militants on both sides of the baby-feeding issue who can list all sorts of esoteric pros and cons. But of much more consequence to you are the seemingly trivial things that will be affected by your choice, things that you will have to live with every day, month after month.

HOW MANY CHOICES YOU'LL
HAVE TO MAKE ON A DAILY BASIS

BOTTLE-FEEDING	**BREAST-FEEDING**
Lots of Choices...	*No Choices...*

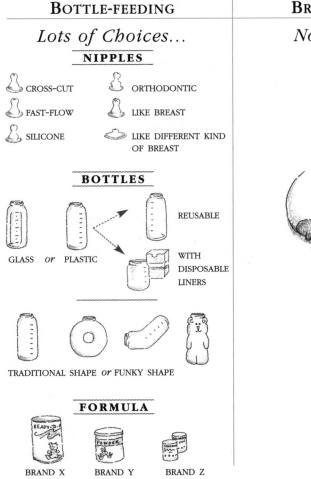

NIPPLES

CROSS-CUT   ORTHODONTIC

FAST-FLOW   LIKE BREAST

SILICONE   LIKE DIFFERENT KIND
                   OF BREAST

BOTTLES

GLASS   *or*   PLASTIC   →   REUSABLE

WITH DISPOSABLE LINERS

TRADITIONAL SHAPE *or* FUNKY SHAPE

FORMULA

BRAND X   BRAND Y   BRAND Z

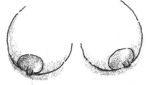

HOW LONG YOU CAN BE GONE FROM HOME

BOTTLE-FEEDING	BREAST-FEEDING
Forever.	*7 minutes, based on a typical nursing cycle:* You fed the baby on the right side; she dozed off for 20 minutes; she woke up and nursed on the left side for 2 minutes and then fell asleep again, and will need to be topped off in 7 minutes.

WHAT YOU CAN EAT FOR DINNER

BOTTLE-FEEDING	BREAST-FEEDING

MARGARITA

SPICY, GARLICKY CHILI

COFFEE

ENCHILADAS

EXTRA-CHOCOLATY BROWNIE

3 GLASSES OF WATER

OATMEAL COOKIES

SALAD

BISCUIT

CHICKEN BREAST   RICE   SPINACH

WHAT'S INVOLVED IN THE PREPARATION

BOTTLE-FEEDING

What you need to have on hand:

FORMULA, READY TO USE OR READY TO MIX

4 4-OUNCE BOTTLES

10 8-OUNCE BOTTLES

10 NIPPLES & RINGS

BOTTLE-CLEANING BRUSH

NIPPLE-CLEANING BRUSH

MEASURING PITCHER

MEASURING CUP

CAN OPENER

MIXING SPOON

TONGS

STERILIZER

Preparation:

Sterilize bottles by scrubbing vigorously with dedicated bottle brush and then placing in rapidly boiling water for five minutes. Wash top of formula can with hot water; rinse and dry. Shake. Use special can opener reserved for formula. Wash can opener immediately after use. Mix formula according to directions with boiled bottled water. Pour formula into bottles. Refrigerate until needed. Run hot water over bottle to warm formula, then use immediately.

Preparation time:

18 minutes, though it seems like 18 hours because the baby has been shrieking the entire time.

BREAST-FEEDING

What you need to have on hand:

BREASTS, 2 (TWO)

Preparation:

UNBUTTON SHIRT

UNLATCH BRA

EXPOSE NIPPLE

Preparation time:

4 SECONDS

OPPORTUNITIES TO CATCH SOME ZZZZZS WHILE FEEDING BABY

BOTTLE-FEEDING	BREAST-FEEDING
Not many.	*Lots.*

WHAT HAPPENS DURING SEX

BOTTLE-FEEDING	BREAST-FEEDING

SPEED-BURPING

"*I* discovered a surefire way to get a burp out of a baby in five seconds or less. Holding the baby vertically, raise and lower him over your head two or three times, then put him against your shoulder and pat his back. Bingo!"

—MARY, MOTHER OF FOUR WELL-BURPED CHILDREN, AGES 2, 4, 6, AND 8

WHAT YOU'LL HAVE TO LISTEN TO YOUR MOTHER-IN-LAW SAYING

BOTTLE-FEEDING	BREAST-FEEDING
"Bring the baby to Grandma . . . See how she likes rocking with Grandma and drinking her bottle? We can see how much milk she's getting. Doesn't that formula look nice and thick! Of course they do say mother's milk is the best thing for babies. But who says this perfect little creature has to have the best? You decided that second-best was good enough and I support that wholeheartedly."	*"I think it's just wonderful that you've decided to breast-feed the baby. Wonderful. But your milk looks kind of thin and watery, doesn't it? Is it supposed to look like that? Are you sure the baby's getting enough? How do you know if she's getting enough? I don't think she's getting enough. But of course, I completely support this decision of yours to breast-feed."*

YOUR WARDROBE OPTIONS

BOTTLE-FEEDING MOM

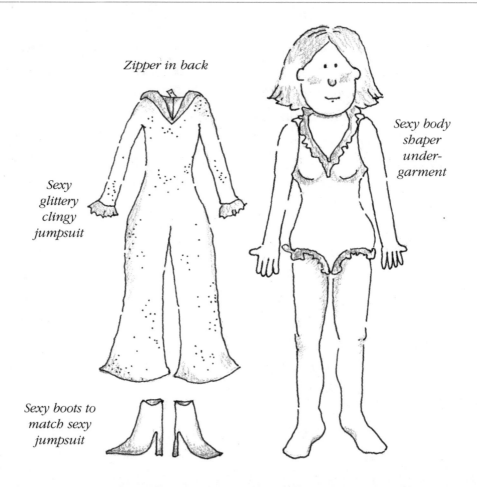

Zipper in back

Sexy glittery clingy jumpsuit

Sexy body shaper under-garment

Sexy boots to match sexy jumpsuit

BREAST-FEEDING MOM

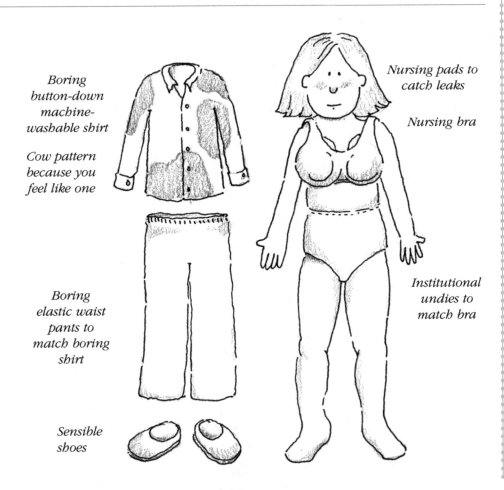

Boring
button-down
machine-
washable shirt

Cow pattern
because you
feel like one

Boring
elastic waist
pants to
match boring
shirt

Sensible
shoes

Nursing pads to
catch leaks

Nursing bra

Institutional
undies to
match bra

STAGES OF BREAST-FEEDING

Breast-feeding evolves over time. Sometimes you and the baby are in sync, and sometimes not. In the "not" category, for example, just when you get comfortable nursing with other people around, the baby decides that Aunt Edna, sitting across the room talking about her day lilies, is much more interesting than your breast. This means only two minutes of actual nursing (in 10-second spurts) takes place during a 20-minute nursing session. There are other times when you and the baby evolve together:

Breast-feeding in public! What is the world coming to?

STAGES OF BREAST-FEEDING

COMFORT LEVEL

STAGE 1   5 MONTHS LATER   **STAGE 2**

Watch for timing how long baby nurses on each side

Nursing chair

Breast-feeding manual

Nursing pillows

Nursing stool

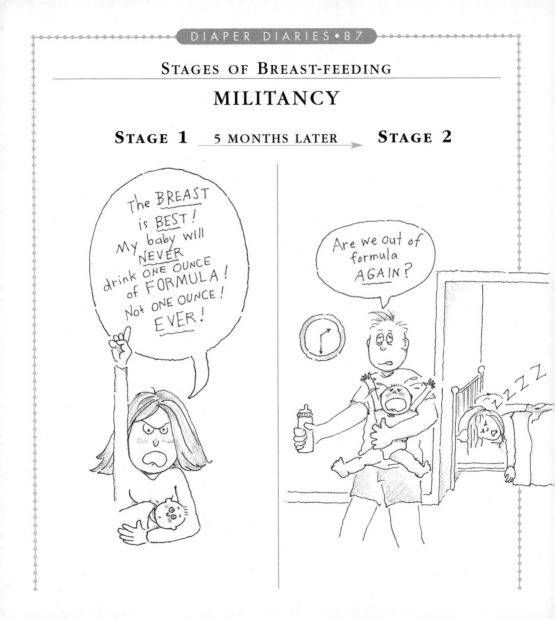

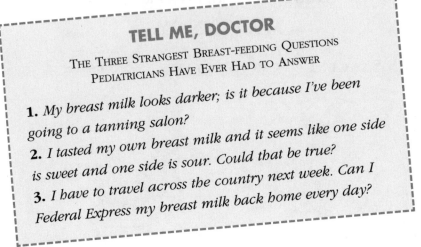

TELL ME, DOCTOR

THE THREE STRANGEST BREAST-FEEDING QUESTIONS
PEDIATRICIANS HAVE EVER HAD TO ANSWER

1. *My breast milk looks darker; is it because I've been going to a tanning salon?*

2. *I tasted my own breast milk and it seems like one side is sweet and one side is sour. Could that be true?*

3. *I have to travel across the country next week. Can I Federal Express my breast milk back home every day?*

BREAST-FEEDING TIPS YOU DON'T REALLY NEED

Attach a safety pin to your bra to remind yourself which side to start nursing on the next time.

RICE CEREAL AND OTHER GOO

It's great when the baby starts eating solids. And not only because you get to videotape all of those dramatic reactions he will have to new tastes and textures, but because this feels like a real milestone. Why, you're practically ready to go to the drive-through at McDonald's and get him a Happy Meal!

There are some startling things about feeding your baby solid foods. One of these is that you put one spoonful of prunes in and the baby will spit three spoonfuls out. Inexplicable from a scientific standpoint, but true nevertheless.

Following are some more amazing things.

ADVICE FROM PEOPLE WITHOUT CHILDREN

"What do you mean he won't eat beets? You wait a coupla hours and try again. When he gets hungry enough, he'll eat 'em!"

THINGS YOU THINK YOUR BABY WOULD LIKE EATING OFF OF

Squeaky clean high-chair tray with stimulating toys suction-cupped onto it

Educational placemat

Sailboat plate from pricey Manhattan department store

THINGS YOUR BABY ACTUALLY WANTS TO EAT OFF OF

Your plate

Floor of rest room in Burger King

Pokey's placemat

THINGS YOU THINK YOUR BABY WOULD LIKE TO EAT

Peas

Slices of banana

Cheerios

Nice, soft bow-tie pasta

Pieces of ripe, juicy watermelon

THINGS YOUR BABY ACTUALLY WANTS TO EAT

Ball of fuzz from under sofa

Dead fly

Old gum

Dirt

Stamp

Mystery knob

Ping Pong ball

HOW TO HANDLE THIS REALITY

Compromise

Experiment with putting food you want the baby to eat in places he will enjoy discovering it: under the coffee table, in the sink, between the sofa cushions, on the edge of the bath tub...

Think positive

▷ The baby will develop a kick-butt immune system from exposure to mega-germs.

▷ The baby will eventually tire of an all-insect diet and will go in search of "real food."

▷ No one ever died from eating dirt.

Get perspective

You won't be packing ping pong balls in his Batman lunch box 5 years from now. He'll catch on.

WASTE MANAGEMENT

There's not really too much variation on what's required of you as a mother right now. You're not trying to convince your son that practicing the piano is more important than watching *The Simpsons*. You're not trying to talk your daughter out of buying a motorcycle and into taking the LSATs. You're feeding, you're burping, and you're changing diapers. But because new moms are so gung-ho, these simple tasks take on grave significance. Every spoonful of strained carrots that goes in and stays there is a victory. Every burp that comes up with just a pat or two on the back is a triumph. Ditto the diaper deal. You—who just a little while back were keeping track of $18 million worth of inventory as your company's controller—are now keeping track of how many BMs the baby made today, and what they looked like. Every normal poop is a sign that your mothering techniques have been successful.

What a difference a few months make, eh?

A POOP BY ANY OTHER NAME

Almost every household has its own names for the private aspects of life. Here are a few for, shall we say, bowel movements:

AWKIES	DOO-DOO	POOP
BOOTYCAKES	DOODY	POOPY-PIE
BMs	NUGS	STINKIES
BROWNIES	NUMBER 2	TINKY-WINKIES
BUM NUGGETS	PLOP	TURDS
CA-CA	POOH-POOH	

POOP VARIETIES

Changing your baby's diaper is like opening a surprise package. You never know what's going to be inside! Will the contents be loose or compact, red or yellow, lumpy or smooth? And just when you think you've been exposed to every possible type of poop, you are startled by yet another variation on the theme. Here's just a sampling:

SWEET AND SQUISHY MUSTARD POOP
One of the unsung benefits of breast-feeding: Baby's poops smell sweet and look like mustard. They also have a low stick-to-the-butt factor, a hearty plus.

LIL' DOLLOP POOP
This one's a teaser. The overpowering odor would lead one to believe that a man-size poop lay within the diaper's folds, when, in reality, one lone poop marble is lurking there. Just add this one to the long list of Baby Incongruities.

FIRE-ENGINE-RED POOP Understandably startling, but usually no cause for alarm. If you are a health nut: Baby ate beets. If you are a junk-food junkie: Baby ate artificially colored breakfast cereal. (Tsk-tsk.)

EXPLOSIVE POOP As if you need more unexpected things to contend with in the first month or two, your baby will shoot out poops machine-gun style with accompanying dramatic sound effects. Thankfully, the Amazing Explosive Poop Phenomenon is short-lived.

SWALLOWED-A-BUTTON POOP Self-explanatory.

LOTS O' RAISINS POOP So often what goes into baby comes out remarkably unaffected by the process of digestion. So it goes with raisins, which you see in that diaper and swear you could pop right back into the box and nobody would be the wiser. (Note: I am *not* recommending that; it was merely an observation.)

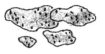

SPECKLED POOP The culprit: bananas. Not to worry . . . unless you have not fed the baby bananas in a while. *Then* you can worry.

SANDY POOP There are two possible explanations. The obvious one is that your baby ate sand. The less obvious one is that your baby ate Cheerios, which look like sand after they've been mushed around in the digestive tract. Choose the more likely scenario.

CORNY POOP Put corn into the raisin category as far as its ability to work its way through baby's digestive tract and emerge with extraordinary likeness to its original state.

BLACK-AS-NIGHT POOP Iron. Maybe the baby's formula is iron-fortified; maybe his vitamin drops have iron in them; maybe he swallowed a cast-iron skillet. But iron's your answer.

QUICK-CHANGE ARTIST

Baby books offer simple directions for changing a baby's diaper:

STEP 1: *Unfasten the old diaper. If it contains a bowel movement, use the unsoiled part of the diaper to wipe away as much of it as possible.*

STEP 2: *Fold and tuck the old diaper under the baby's bottom as you wipe the baby from front to back with baby wipes.*

STEP 3: *As you lift the baby's bottom to clean it, slip the old diaper out and a new one under him.*

STEP 4: *Allow baby's bottom to air-dry before applying ointment and fastening the new diaper.*

Unfortunately, the underlying assumption here is that you are at home with your changing table and a myriad of useful supplies at hand. Very often this is not the case.

HERE ARE MORE REALISTIC DIAPER-CHANGING SITUATIONS

In a restaurant, inconspicuously

In the car (always inclement weather)

In church (you will be forgiven)

In a store, behind the DVD sale display

TALES FROM THE FIELD

THE WORST PLACE I'VE EVER HAD TO CHANGE A DIAPER

"*My husband and I decided to take our eight-month-old twins on a three-hour bus tour of Atlanta (not our best parenting decision). The bus stopped at this circular, rotating theater where we were supposed to watch a reenactment of the Battle of Atlanta. The minute the lights went out and the seats started moving, Thomas freaked out and let loose with a very smelly BM. So as the cannons were blasting and soldiers were collapsing, I whipped off the dirty diaper and stuck on a clean one. Unfortunately, the seats were rotating, but the smell stayed put, which meant that as people rotated to where we'd been, they were overwhelmed by the smell of poop. You could hear them react as they hit the stinky spot. And to make things worse, the lights came on just as I was triumphantly handing the dirty diaper over to my husband, so it was very clear who was responsible.*"

—Jane

"*I had taken my two children to the park. The baby needed a change, so I stuck her on the picnic table closest to the playground and proceeded to change her very messy diaper. When I was done, I turned around with the baby and the dirty diaper and came face-to-face with a family holding a cooler full of food, staring at me in total disgust.*"

—Lisa

"*We were on a hike with the baby when he made such a huge mess in his diaper that we had to take it off. Unfortunately, I had run out of wipes and clean diapers. So I wiped him off as well as I could with the dirty diaper, washed off his little bottom in a stream, and then concocted a 'diaper' using my underpants, a couple of sanitary pads (thank goodness I had remembered to pack those), and a plastic bag. Not pretty, but it worked!*"
—HELEN

"*My worst diaper-changing experience was at a racetrack where my brother-in-law was competing in a car race. I was watching seven kids—all of his kids and mine. Just a few laps into the race, his youngest had one of those blow-out diapers where yellow poop just shoots right up the baby's back. I had to haul the whole group of kids through the stands and all the way back to the parking lot where the baby's things were. I changed him on the tailgate of my brother's truck with commentary provided by a bunch of guys who had just parked their motorcycles. We all trooped back to our seats, and two minutes later, wouldn't you know it, the baby had another blow-out.*"
—CHERI

"*My son was in the partially potty-trained stage when we were forced to bring him along to a dinner party because our baby-sitter cancelled. No one else in the group had children. Just as we sat down to eat, Nicky wandered in from where he had been watching a video. I immediately knew he had pooped in his training diaper, so I made an excuse and left the table to deal with it. I had nothing to change him into, so I stuck his pants back on, prayed for the best, and returned to the table with an excuse about the video being scary. Unfortunately, about five minutes later, he reappeared in the dining room. It turns out he had not finished pooping and he was holding the evidence in his hand for everyone to see.*"
—JAN

SELF-JUSTIFICATION

We all know that disposable diapers take 109 years to biodegrade and that cloth diapers are more "natural" and even have a kind of retro chic. But real life sometimes interferes with our lofty intentions and we go for what's easy. Here's how real moms rationalize using disposable diapers (even if they always vote for Ralph Nader whenever he's running):

"*I just recycle everything else, even the little clear plastic windows on envelopes.*"
—ANNETTE

"*I used cloth diapers for the first two weeks and the baby got a bad diaper rash. I was dying to use disposables anyway, so I blamed the rash on the diapers and switched!*"
—LEIGH

"*I try to use as few as possible by leaving every diaper on for a really, really long time.*"
—MANDY

"*I pick up other people's trash at the park and figure it's a wash.*"
—BETH

"*Hey, way before disposable diapers start clogging up the landfills, global warming will have killed us all off anyway.*"
—KERI

"*Don't you have to use big pins with cloth diapers? I mean, isn't that dangerous with the way babies squirm when you're changing them?*"
—KELLY

"*I figure I'm not using all that hot water, detergent, and bleach to clean the cloth diapers, right?*"
—ELLEN

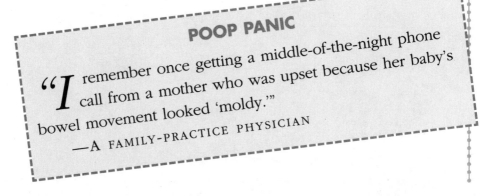

POOP PANIC

"*I remember once getting a middle-of-the-night phone call from a mother who was upset because her baby's bowel movement looked 'moldy.'*"
—A FAMILY-PRACTICE PHYSICIAN

THE NEW YOU

Like my friend Mary says, "It's all about attitude." Keep that in mind when you take inventory of the damage done to your various body parts. You can lament the saggy belly and the stretch marks that criss-cross your hips like a crazy map to nowhere, or you can focus on the accomplishments of your remarkable uterus. You can obsess about your shrinking vocabulary and nonexistent memory or take pride in your newfound patience and your capacity for boundless love. It's your call, but Mary's usually right.

NASTY LITTLE SURPRISES OF NEW MOTHERHOOD

Once you take stock of your postpartum body, you're going to want a guarantee, in writing, that this child whose incubation and birth wreaked such havoc on you from head to toe will grow up to be some sort of Albert Einstein/Mother Teresa/Bill Gates combo. In the event that you are unable to secure such a guarantee, just do what other mothers do: Develop the ability to perceive your average child as remarkably gifted in all areas, thus making any pain and suffering worthwhile.

TEMPORARY DAMAGE

In a nutshell: You've got all of that nice, thick pregnancy hair falling out in clumps; you've got grotesquely huge, leaky boobs; you've got a Pillsbury Dough Boy belly; you've got a bloated face; and you may still have to contend with the aftermath of that agonizingly painful episiotomy or C-section. (*Note to self:* Never have octuplets, because you really wouldn't want to have your postpartum picture in the newspaper.) But all these conditions will eventually go away. Not so with the following:

PERMANENT DAMAGE

YOUR FEET ARE BIGGER. Why this is, no one knows. Or at least no one has told *me*. But I think I also got shorter after I had kids, so maybe there is some sort of sliding downward and outward that occurs. In any event, the upside is you get to go out and buy all new shoes.

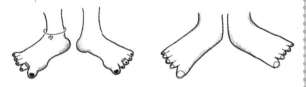

Feet, prepregnancy   *Same feet, postbaby*

YOU WET YOUR PANTS WHEN YOU SNEEZE. This has something to do with your traumatized pelvic floor. You have three options: You can do something called

Kegel exercises to tighten up all of that internal hardware; you can learn techniques to stop a sneeze when you feel one coming on; or you can just wear a pad in your underpants.

YOUR BELLY BUTTON IS SAD AND DROOPY. During the final months of pregnancy, your belly button was stretched to the point of popping out like the "ready" button on a Perdue chicken. And after you gave birth, it became shriveled up like a toothless old mouth. It just doesn't have the rebound capabilities that some of the other parts of you do. Thankfully, once you're past the age of 17, you don't have a lot of opportunities to show off your belly button to the general public. And just think of all the money you'll save on belly-button accessories.

YOU'VE BEEN STRETCHED, AND YOU'VE GOT GROOVES TO PROVE IT. You probably have lovely reddish-purplish lines, appropriately named stretch marks, spanning every area that saw an excessive stretching of skin. Usually this means your tummy, and sometimes your hips, breasts, and butt. Eventually, the reddish streaks turn silverish. (That sounds prettier than it actually is.) You own these guys forever, so learn to love 'em.

YOU HAVE VARICOSE VEINS LIKE YOUR MOTHER. People think of varicose veins as leg decorations, but actually they can pop out anywhere. (Here's a bit of trivia: Technically, hemorrhoids are varicose veins of the rectal area.) Progesterone and blood pressure are factors, but if you're looking for something you can blame on your 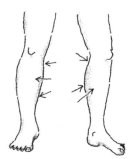 mother, go with this (there's a convenient genetic component). When your flock is complete, you can have surgery and look (almost) as good as new.

ADVICE FROM PEOPLE WITHOUT CHILDREN

"Oh, you just get a little exercise and skip those late-night snacks and your body'll bounce back in no time!"

YOUR BRAIN, THEN AND NOW

Your brain is divided into sections according to subject matter, much like a bookstore.

HERE WAS YOUR BRAIN BEFORE

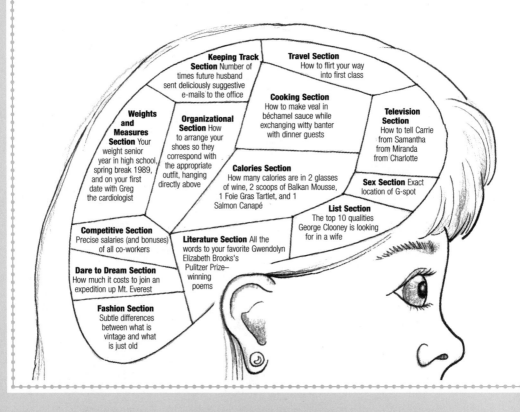

Keeping Track Section Number of times future husband sent deliciously suggestive e-mails to the office

Travel Section How to flirt your way into first class

Cooking Section How to make veal in béchamel sauce while exchanging witty banter with dinner guests

Weights and Measures Section Your weight senior year in high school, spring break 1989, and on your first date with Greg the cardiologist

Organizational Section How to arrange your shoes so they correspond with the appropriate outfit, hanging directly above

Television Section How to tell Carrie from Samantha from Miranda from Charlotte

Calories Section How many calories are in 2 glasses of wine, 2 scoops of Balkan Mousse, 1 Foie Gras Tartlet, and 1 Salmon Canapé

Sex Section Exact location of G-spot

List Section The top 10 qualities George Clooney is looking for in a wife

Competitive Section Precise salaries (and bonuses) of all co-workers

Literature Section All the words to your favorite Gwendolyn Elizabeth Brooks's Pulitzer Prize–winning poems

Dare to Dream Section How much it costs to join an expedition up Mt. Everest

Fashion Section Subtle differences between what is vintage and what is just old

The sections themselves don't change once you have a baby, but the information contained within changes dramatically. Studies have shown that you can never get your old brain back.

HERE IS YOUR BRAIN NOW

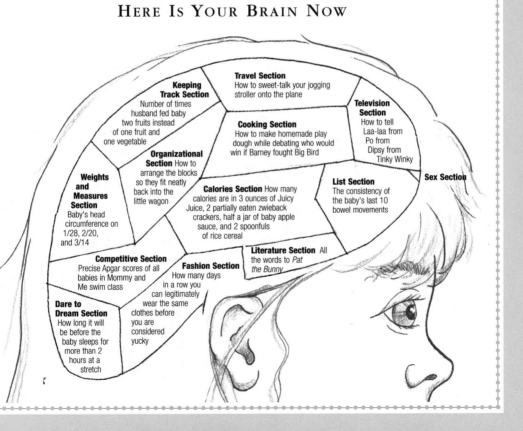

Travel Section How to sweet-talk your jogging stroller onto the plane

Keeping Track Section Number of times husband fed baby two fruits instead of one fruit and one vegetable

Television Section How to tell Laa-laa from Po from Dipsy from Tinky Winky

Cooking Section How to make homemade play dough while debating who would win if Barney fought Big Bird

Organizational Section How to arrange the blocks so they fit neatly back into the little wagon

Weights and Measures Section Baby's head circumference on 1/28, 2/20, and 3/14

Calories Section How many calories are in 3 ounces of Juicy Juice, 2 partially eaten zwieback crackers, half a jar of baby apple sauce, and 2 spoonfuls of rice cereal

List Section The consistency of the baby's last 10 bowel movements

Sex Section

Competitive Section Precise Apgar scores of all babies in Mommy and Me swim class

Fashion Section How many days in a row you can legitimately wear the same clothes before you are considered yucky

Literature Section All the words to *Pat the Bunny*

Dare to Dream Section How long it will be before the baby sleeps for more than 2 hours at a stretch

BOOBY PROGRESSION

From Perky to Pendulous

Find your boobies under the category "Original Boobies." Then follow them through the stages of pregnancy and nursing to see what they evolve into. As you will observe, no matter how spectacular they were in their "original" state, boobies look pretty much the same after their owners have had a baby or two. (Which is good news—or sweet revenge—for those of us who weren't centerfold material to begin with.)

ORIGINAL BOOBIES	EARLY PREGNANCY	LATE PREGNANCY	NURSING	AFTER BABY STOPS NURSING

JELLY BELLY

Select the image that most closely resembles your new belly:

- ☐ RISEN BREAD DOUGH
- ☐ A JUST-POPPED BALLOON
- ☐ HOMEMADE PLAY DOUGH
- ☐ JELLO MOLD GONE WRONG

- ☐ A SINGLE BED WEARING A KING-SIZE FITTED SHEET
- ☐ FLUBBER

A QUESTION OF BABY FAT

How long can those extra pounds you accumulated during pregnancy accurately be referred to as "baby fat"? It is a complex, multifaceted, and very individual question, with a number of variables to consider.

Here is a basic guideline:

NOW IT IS "BABY FAT"

NOW IT IS JUST "FAT"

DAILY DIET—
BEST INTENTIONS VS. REAL LIFE

You know that the best way to make sure that you eat a healthy diet is to have a plan in place ahead of time. And you know that the best way to keep track of what you're eating is to keep a food diary (doesn't Oprah tell us this all the time?). So… you have a plan, and you are keeping track. The only problem is that there's a slight difference between what you *planned on* eating and what you *ended up* eating…

THE PLAN	THE REALITY
	My Food Diary
BREAKFAST ½ grapefruit 1 slice wheat toast 1 poached egg	7:35 a.m. ½ grapefruit dry wheat toast (saving the egg calories for later!) 9:15 a.m. 2 partially chewed Zwieback Crackers and ½ cup Cheerios / raisins Snack (otherwise it would have gone to waste)

MID-MORNING
SNACK
1 small apple

LUNCH
Small salad
with low-fat
dressing

4 Saltines

diet soda

10:40 a.m. 2 apples (they were really, really small)

10:55 a.m. Just a few potato chips, crumbs really (so that I could throw away the bag and make more room in the pantry)

11:15 a.m. The THINNEST slice of coffee cake that it was possible to cut (the next-door neighbor just brought it over and I had to be polite and try some)

11:25 a.m. One more thin slice just to even up the ends and to show my neighbor how much I liked it

11:55 a.m. A slice of leftover pizza (no time to make a salad; also, no lettuce or tomatoes in refrig)

1:20 p.m. Mixed nuts (baby fell asleep nursing and that's all I could reach)

MID-AFTERNOON

SNACK

2 graham crackers

1 cup skim milk

DINNER

Skinless chicken breast, broiled

½ cup spinach

small baked potato

plain tea

AFTER-DINNER

SNACK

1 cup low-fat microwave popcorn

3:35 p.m. One more teeny tiny piece of the coffee cake

4:45 p.m. One Beef Stroganoff Lean Cuisine

6:10 p.m. One Fettucini Alfredo Lean Cuisine (I think these things have negative calories — I'm hungrier AFTER I eat them from all the chewing)

7:30 p.m. Three little bites of Kung Pao Chicken (take out from 2 nights ago — otherwise I'd have had to throw it out)

9:15 p.m. One Oreo

9:20 p.m. Another Oreo

9:30 p.m. Two more Oreos

9:35 p.m. 3 more Oreos

11:55 p.m. Fritos and Onion dip (because I blew it anyway. But at MIDNIGHT I am going to start fresh and this time I'LL STICK TO MY PLAN!)

BABY BLUES

Why, when you have been blessed with an adorable, healthy baby, are you *sad*? Shouldn't you be *ecstatic*? What's *wrong* with you?

Let's assess, shall we?

REASONS TO FEEL HAPPY

❑ I have an adorable, healthy baby.

REASONS TO FEEL DEPRESSED

❑ I have never been so exhausted in my entire life.

❑ I'm fat.

❑ I have to wear maternity clothes because nothing else fits and I am *sick* of my maternity clothes.

❑ Because I am wearing maternity clothes, people keep asking me when the baby is due.

❑ I'm leaking everywhere.

❑ I don't think I'll ever want to have sex again and my husband will leave me for his perky-boobed, barely-out-of-puberty secretary.

❑ It seems like I work all day and get nothing done.

❑ My house is a total mess.

❑ There are days when all the baby does is cry and poop.

❑ The babies on TV commercials are all happier than mine.

❑ I miss work where I actually did the things on my to-do list.

❑ My old friends don't understand what I'm going through.

❑ I'm not going to be able to make any new friends because I'm fat and miserable. Even I wouldn't want to be my friend.

❑ My mother-in-law is driving me nuts.

❑ I'm afraid I'll do something wrong and ruin this poor little baby.

❑ My husband is a better mother than I am. If he had breasts, he would be better at breast-feeding than I am.

❑ I've changed my mind. I'd rather have a kitten.

ADVICE FROM PEOPLE WITHOUT CHILDREN

"Oh, for goodness sake, just snap out of it."

WHEN THERE'S ONLY TIME
FOR ONE OF YOU TO LOOK GOOD

ZZZZZZZZZZZ

Before baby, you took sleep for granted: It was there when you wanted it. But after baby, sleep takes on a whole new significance in your life.

You crave sleep, you obsess about it, you would pay handsomely for a full night of it, and you do strange things when deprived of it. Infants may *technically* sleep 20 hours a day, but they do it 10 minutes at a time while making strange, at-death's-door kind of choking and gurgling noises.

Hardly conducive to you catching up on *your* zzzzs.

But the good news is that this situation is temporary. You can look forward to a respite from sleep deprivation during the brief period after your child stops being afraid of the dark and before she starts asking for help with algebra homework at 11:15 P.M.

ADVICE FROM PEOPLE WITHOUT CHILDREN

"Babies sleep all the time. Just sleep when the baby does and you'll get plenty of rest."

SWEET DREAMS

For the baby who scoffs at your attempts to put her to sleep by the traditional rock-and-hum method, here are some more unusual things you can try that just might work:

1. *Vacuum with the baby against you in a Snugli or sling.*

WHY THIS WORKS: You might think the baby likes the movement, the white noise, and the closeness to you. Nope. It's just that given the choice between watching you vacuum or sleeping, the baby—like any sane human being—will generally opt for sleep.

2. *Tape a life-size photo of your smiling face to the inside of the crib.*

WHY THIS WORKS: The baby relaxes and nods off, content in the knowledge that she is keeping you awake, which is what she really wants anyway.

3. *Put the baby in the stroller and walk her around* inside *the house.*

WHY THIS WORKS: It's not the motion that does it; you're basically just boring her to sleep.

4. Play a tape recording of you singing lullabies.

WHY THIS WORKS: This works by the Armadillo Theory: A creature will play dead in the hopes that the torture will stop.

5. Put the baby (in her baby seat) on top of the washing machine or dryer while it is going.

WHY THIS WORKS: No, it's not the comforting vibrations of the washer or dryer that calm the baby. The baby *pretends* to be asleep because she hears you muttering, "Does this plain, white sock match this white one or this white one?" and she is afraid you are going to expect some worthwhile input from her. But often, pretending to sleep leads to

the real thing. Worth a try.

6. Swaddle the baby or put rolled-up blankets on either side of her.

WHY THIS WORKS: Unable to roll over or move any significant body part in a meaningful way, the baby falls asleep in an attempt to temporarily escape the misery of her situation.

7. Put a hat and socks on her.

WHY THIS WORKS: The baby thinks you are taking her somewhere so she will fall asleep in an attempt to foil the plan (see Grocery Shopping With the Baby, page 166).

8. *Drive around the neighborhood in the car.*

WHY THIS WORKS: See previous entry.

9. *Have a consistent bedtime routine.*

WHY THIS WORKS: Here we are employing the Uncle Charlie Theory of Sleep Cycles Based on Long-standing Habit: Everyone knows that after he has eaten dinner and told the same old back-on-the-farm stories over coffee, Uncle Charlie will pat Aunt Betty on the butt, retire to the den, and fall asleep on the couch. Substitute "baby" for "Uncle Charlie," "has a warm bath and is rocked and sung to" for "told the same old back-on-the-farm stories over coffee," etc., and you understand the theory.

10. *Put a clock with a loud "tick-tock" near the baby's bed.*

WHY THIS WORKS: It's true that the ticking of the clock, like a heartbeat, is a soothing sound to a baby. But that's not why this puts the baby to sleep. Suddenly aware of the passage of time, the baby doesn't want to waste time fighting you on the whole nap deal. She wants to fall asleep right away and get the nap over with so that she can embrace the rest of this glorious day that will never come again. Carpe diem!

11. *Just before bedtime, toss her favorite blanket into the dryer to make it nice and toasty warm.*

WHY THIS WORKS: The baby thinks she's dozing on a sunny beach in the Caribbean. Prepare for a real howl when she awakens to a Winnie-the-Pooh mural instead of swaying palm trees.

12. *Try to fool the baby by yawning and acting sleepy yourself.*

WHY THIS WORKS: The baby, embarrassed on your behalf for such a lame fake-out attempt, will humor you by closing her eyes. "Yeah, right," she thinks, "like Mom is really going to fall asleep right now, when she is dying to put me down so she can watch *Friends.* But I'd better cooperate or she'll make an even bigger fool out of herself by climbing into the crib with me. Jeesh."

YAWN

CRAZY DAZE

STORIES FROM THE FIRST WEEKS OF PARENTHOOD

Do you remember reading about the father who put his infant daughter (in her car seat) on his car roof as he buckled up his toddler, and then drove away with the baby on the roof?! Yikes! Thankfully, the baby, who eventually slid off the roof, landed upright and unharmed in the road. Reflecting on my reaction (okay, okay, *over*reaction) when my husband put our daughter's undershirt on backwards a couple of times, I don't even want to speculate as to what that guy's wife said to him when he got home.

That may be an extreme example, but nearly everyone has a Sleep Deprivation Nightmare Story from the first days or weeks of new parenthood. Even dads are susceptible, though moms, already reeling from the aftershocks of childbirth, usually bear the brunt of the exhaustion.

Here are some other strange tales from those initial hazy, crazy first days of new parenthood.

CUSTOMIZING THE CAR

Marie buckled her three-month-old son John into his car seat one morning to head to a play group. She checked to make sure she had all the things she might need for the morning's outing: extra diapers and wipes, extra clothes, pacifier, blanket, etc. As she got into the driver's seat, she tried to imagine what she may have forgotten to bring for the baby.  Finally satisfied that she had remembered everything, she turned the key and backed out of the driveway. Unfortunately, she had forgotten to shut her car door, which caught on a sturdy tree and bent in half.

DON'T FREEZE THE KEYS!

Christine was very proud when she returned from grocery shopping with her baby—she had not forgotten one item on her list and had made it through the store with no major meltdowns. She put her groceries away, got the baby down for a nap, and rested for an hour or so. When she and the baby woke up, she decided to drive to the park. But she couldn't find her car keys. Two hours later, after a thorough search of the house, she was stumped: no keys. It wasn't until she got herself a bowl of ice cream two days later that she discovered where she had put the keys—in the freezer.

ON THE VALUE
OF COUNTING HEADS

Evie has five children and, until number five, had no Sleep Deprivation Stories to tell. But now she has one her husband won't let her forget. Her infant daughter was just a few weeks old when she and her sister decided to take all of their children for a quick trip to a nearby beach. When they returned, Evie saw her husband, who had come home from work, standing in the doorway, his arms folded across his chest. When she got out of the car, he asked her, "Where's the baby?" She flung open the door of the van and searched the little faces in the back of the car, quickly realizing that the baby's was not among them. "Oh no!" she shrieked, panic setting in. "I don't know where she is!" "I do," her husband said. "She's in her crib. You must have forgotten to take her with you because she was napping. Thankfully, she still is. Next time you might want to count heads before you leave the house."

SLIP-SLIDIN' AWAY

Gary offered to hold his four-month-old son when he and his wife began a long plane trip. They had been up a lot the night before with the baby, and both were delighted and grateful when the motion and hum of the plane's engine soothed the baby to sleep. They reclined in their seats, hoping to relax during the flight. All at once, Gary was awakened by a flight attendant poking him in the shoulder. "I think this belongs to you," he said, handing him the baby, who was gazing around curiously. Gary had fallen asleep, and the baby had rolled off his lap and ended up under the seat in front of him.

WONDERING WHY HE'S WANDERING

After a midnight feeding and diaper changing, Cathy quietly carried her sleeping baby back to the master bedroom, where the bassinet was. Finding it too dark to navigate across the room, she whispered to her husband, "Could you please switch on the nightlight?" He stirred, but didn't move toward the light. So she repeated the request. He finally stood up, naked, and walked out of the room. Puzzled, Cathy waited as she listened to his footsteps in the hall, then going down the stairs. A few minutes later, the outside lights went on. She tiptoed over to the window and peeked out. There was her husband, wandering around the yard, still naked. After about five minutes, the outside lights went off, he returned to their room, and got back in bed, all without having turned on the nightlight. In the morning, he had no memory of his naked nighttime stroll across the yard.

THE 10 BEST THINGS ABOUT BEING UP WITH THE BABY AT 2:15 A.M.

Let's consider this up-all-night-with-a-wide-eyed-baby thing from the glass-is-half-full perspective.

1. You can air-dry your nipples without worrying that the UPS man will peek in the porch window.

2. You can finally return your friends' e-mails congratulating you on the baby's arrival and get lots of sympathy when they see what time is on your e-mail.

3. You can watch reruns of *Saved by the Bell* (not really a bad little show, especially when watched in a state of near exhaustion).

4. You can call your friends who live in different time zones.

5. You can pick the cashews out of the mixed nuts without being seen.

6. You can turn on the radio and move the dial around and see if you can tune in stations from other countries.

7. You can have anything you want to eat. Food eaten between 1 and 5 A.M. doesn't really count calorie-wise because . . . well, just because.

8. You have the chance to finally finger the critter who's been getting into your garbage can.

9. You can bone up on the constellations.

10. You can put something in the Crock-Pot and it will be ready to eat at lunchtime.

LULLABIES

As you are rocking her, it's natural to want to sing your baby to sleep. But so many of the standard lullabies are, shall we say, a bit off-putting. From telling Aunt Rhody about her dead goose to the ladybug's nightmare-inducing house fire, traditional lullabies are in need of a major overhaul. Perhaps the most horrifying lullaby is the classic "Rock-a-Bye Baby" in which the bough breaks, sending the baby hurtling toward the ground, cradle and all.

Uh oh.

Some first and second graders have graciously provided new and improved endings to our most familiar rocking tune. Feel free to substitute one of their endings for the standard one.

Rock-a-bye, baby, in the treetop.
When the wind blows, the cradle will rock;
When the bough breaks, the cradle will fall,
And ...

... down will come baby to shop in the mall. —OWEN

... baby will bounce like a big rubber ball. —AMELIA

... the baby is so tall that he won't get hurt at all. —RYAN C.

... the baby will swing from vine to vine like Tarzan. —DMITRI

... the baby will start bawling but he's really OK. —TIM

... a very pretty horse is waiting under the tree to
catch the baby. —LACEY

... the baby rolls and rolls and rolls and is fine. —RYAN W.

... the baby will only break his or her kneecap. —JOSH

... Mommy is there to catch her and figures out not to
stick her up in a tree anymore. —JESSICA

THE JOYS OF THE BABY MONITOR

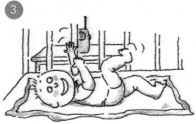

DOCTOR, DOCTOR

Initially, because your maternal confidence is a little shaky, you will rely heavily on your pediatrician for advice and reassurance. It won't be long, though, before you are the expert on your baby. Then, *you* will be telling *the doctor* that the baby has an ear infection and what medications he can tolerate.

In the meantime, though, there is the all-important pediatrician selection process as well as the first few traumatic doctor's appointments. Here are some survival tips.

CHOOSING THE PERFECT PEDIATRICIAN

So many factors will influence what pediatrician or family doctor you choose—the type of practice, hospital affiliation, credentials, and where the office is located. You'd also like to know if the nurse is nice, because you'll be seeing a lot more of her than you will the doctor, and if anyone ever disinfects all of the toys that dozens of sick little children drool and sneeze on in the waiting room everyday.

But what you really want to do is test drive the doctor. Here's the scenario: Your baby is acting fussy and has the sniffles and a low fever. Here's how each of your three finalists responds. Which doctor would you choose for your baby?

ADVICE FROM PEOPLE WITHOUT CHILDREN

"Never mind what you think. Listen to the doctor. He knows a lot more about your baby than you do."

DR. McPHEE

- Kindly, slow-moving old gent who favors tried-and-true remedies
- Has treated 1,304,509 babies in his 37 years of practice
- Takes an I've-seen-it-all approach
- Still makes house calls

HIS RESPONSE: *"Your little fella just has a cold. Nothing to worry about, nothing at all. Seen many a cold in my day. He'll be just fine. Let's wait and see how he's doing in a couple of days. Shall we put a sticker on his sweater that says he's been a good baby?"*

DR. BOB

- Gives out his home phone number
- Lived and practiced among Native Americans
- Hugs all children after asking their permission
- Will go to extremes to avoid prescribing antibiotics

HIS RESPONSE: *"Poor little guy has a cold. I'm thinking elderberry or gingerroot for the congestion; acupuncture might help the clogged ears. Here's some information on folk remedies. Of course, Native Americans would recommend purging in a sweat lodge, followed by shamanic healing using the medicine wheel and the sacred hoop. Would that be something you'd consider?"*

DR. THROCKS-WELDON

- Reads every issue of every medical journal and attends every pediatric medical conference everywhere
- Is quick to treat any symptom; her motto is "Let's nip this in the bud"
- Is okay with the idea of toddlers on leashes

HER RESPONSE: *"Your little one has a cold. If his symptoms don't improve within 24 hours, you can fill these prescriptions. Administer the first one every four hours; for the second, put two drops in each nostril six times a day; and the third one is to be applied to the skin three times a day for a vaporizing effect. Good luck."*

ALL IN A DAY'S WORK

Here are the three strangest questions my friend Joy, a pediatrician, heard in a single day:

"My baby is very wiggly. Should I be worried?"

"Every time I feed my baby solid food, he sneezes. Feeding him is getting to be a very messy experience. How can I prevent him from sneezing?"

"My baby doesn't seem to like other 'real' babies, but he does like the baby on the Gerber cereal box. If I put the box in front of him, he babbles to the baby like he's having a conversation. Is something wrong with him?"

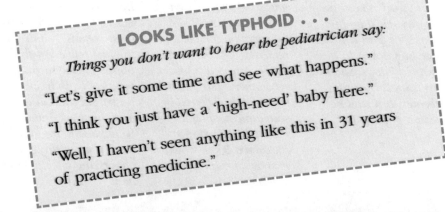

LOOKS LIKE TYPHOID . . .

Things you don't want to hear the pediatrician say:

"Let's give it some time and see what happens."

"I think you just have a 'high-need' baby here."

"Well, I haven't seen anything like this in 31 years of practicing medicine."

WELL-BABY CHECKUP

A Typical Experience

You dress up the baby in one of her cutest outfits (the one with 24 snaps and 14 buttons and a matching bonnet and booties) and head for the doctor's office.

As you are sitting in the reception area listening for your name, you hear your baby's name being called and are suddenly struck by the fact that she is her own person with her own appointment and you are really just there to carry her from place to place. An epiphany, really.

You are ushered into the examination room where the nurse instructs you to remove the baby's outfit, without first commenting on its cuteness. She leaves the room.

You remove the outfit, with its 24 snaps and 14 buttons. You wonder whether or not to remove the diaper, and decide not to, but worry that the nurse will scold you when she returns and sees that the diaper is still on. The baby starts crying because she is cold.

Forty-two minutes later, the baby stops crying and falls asleep.

Forty-four minutes later, the nurse reappears and calls the baby by the wrong name, significantly eroding your initial confidence in her abilities. She also tells you to take the diaper off.

She opens and closes the baby's chart in less than three seconds, then unceremoniously plunks your naked, sleeping baby on an ice-cold, metal scale from the 1920s. The baby wakes up and starts to cry and flail. As your baby teeters precariously, you reach over to keep her from tumbling onto the floor and the nurse scolds you for potentially messing up the weight reading.

Suddenly, the nurse moves into slow motion, pushing the weight bar on the scale 2 millionths of an inch to the left, then 3 millionths of an inch to the right, and then back and forth again six times, all while the baby flails and screams.

Finally satisfied that she has determined the baby's weight to within $\frac{1}{250}$ of a pound, the nurse allows you to grab your teetering baby and try to calm her down.

The nurse scribbles in the chart. She takes much longer than it would take to write down a number, and you wonder if she is making comments like "mother seems neurotic" or "mother left diaper on when I asked her to take off *all* of baby's clothes."

She then takes the baby from you again and lays her on the exam table covered with crinkly paper. The baby starts squirming and crying louder, seemingly unable to connect increased squirming with increased crinkling.

As both crinkling and crying escalate, the nurse asks you to hold your baby down while she wraps the baby's head with a tape measure. The baby looks at you as if horrified by your participation in this medical torture.

Then the nurse stretches the baby out like you'd pull taffy to figure out how long she is. She scribbles for several more minutes.

DIAPER RASH: IS THE CURE WORSE THAN THE CONDITION?

"I couldn't find anything to cure my son's diaper rash. None of the usual creams and lotions did anything to make it better. One day, my mother-in-law brought over this cream that she told me to try and it worked! I was thrilled! When the cream was gone, I asked her where she had gotten it so I could buy more and she told me that she had picked it up at the farm-supply store. It was supposed to be used on infected cow udders!"

—HANNAH

She shows you where the baby falls on the height-weight chart, the Ultimate Standard of Baby Size. You earn that coveted 50th percentile, relieving you of Christmas-future nightmares that your daughter will be either destined to play the littlest elf in the pageant every year or will be the only one able to put the star on top of the tree without standing on a ladder.

The doctor finally comes in and asks you all sorts of tricky questions. You are afraid that if you answer incorrectly, he will take the baby and give her to another mother who had better answers.

Then he pokes the baby all over on the crinkly paper and asks you some more questions about the baby's head control and hand use and social interaction and you are wishing this was like high school where they told you ahead of time what things would be covered on the test.

The doctor then says he will give the baby immunizations today that he refers to by *Star Wars* kinds of names: DTaP, IPV, Hib, Hep-B4, and PCV7.

He gives you one minute and 13 seconds to read 27 pages of information about everything that has ever gone wrong after a baby has been given a shot.

Then he warns you that common reactions to the vaccine range from excessive crankiness (which you're thinking you probably wouldn't notice) to excessive sleepiness (which you're kind of hoping for).

He allows you 24 seconds to read another stack of papers that say, essentially: "This shot could prevent some horrible disease in the future or cause one. The baby could die from this shot in five minutes or sometime next week. She may have seizures, convulsions, and brain damage—or not. Sign here."

The nurse says that you should have given the baby Tylenol before the appointment so that the shot would not cause her as much discomfort, but you're thinking that you should have taken a tranquilizer so that the shot wouldn't cause *you* so much discomfort.

The doctor jabs the baby with what you hope is the correct needle and, as the baby screams, he tells you what advances the baby should be making in the next month or two. But all you hear is "baby," "legs," and "if" because the baby's mouth is in direct contact with your ear.

Then he asks if you have any questions and you say no.

The doctor and nurse leave you alone in the exam room to redress your hysterical baby.

As you leave with 15 nifty germs you didn't have when you arrived, your fingers crossed for "excessive sleepiness," you remember the 17 very important questions you meant to ask.

DAYS OF
OUR LIVES

Your once predictable daily life has been turned on its head. You find yourself trying to fall asleep at 10:30 A.M. because the baby's napping, then raiding the refrigerator at 3:15 A.M. because that's when the baby wants to eat. Whatever it is that you need is inevitably behind the door with the baby latch or on the other side of the baby gate. A simple trip to the grocery store requires as much foresight and planning as a week's vacation in Europe.

And that's not all. Now weekends are a thing of the past: Saturday is a lot like Tuesday, but without *All My Children* and *Oprah*.

But it won't take long for you to adjust to Daily Life That Revolves Around Cranky Little Person. You just need to change the way you clean the house, cook, run errands, drive the car, and just about everything else. You did create a life recently, though, so these other things should be pretty easy.

WHY YOU LABEL BABY PHOTOS

TODAY

"I'll never forget this moment. . . . She looks like a little angel. . . ."

20 YEARS FROM NOW

"Who the heck is this?"

YOUR HOUSE—
BEFORE AND AFTER

Everyone else looking at your living room will see the same couch, the same coffee table, the same rug, the same . . . well, you get the idea. But not you. Not the *New Mom* you. The New Mom you sees everything through New Mom Eyes, which are drastically different from Childless Gal Eyes.

HERE'S HOW YOU SAW YOUR LIVING ROOM BEFORE YOU HAD A BABY

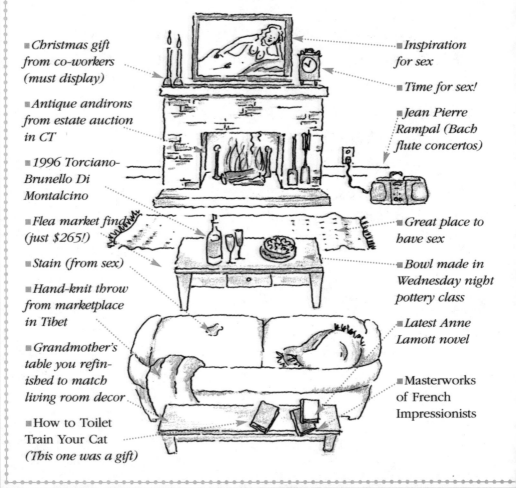

- *Christmas gift from co-workers (must display)*
- *Antique andirons from estate auction in CT*
- *1996 Torciano-Brunello Di Montalcino*
- *Flea market find (just $265!)*
- *Stain (from sex)*
- *Hand-knit throw from marketplace in Tibet*
- *Grandmother's table you refinished to match living room decor*
- How to Toilet Train Your Cat *(This one was a gift)*

- *Inspiration for sex*
- *Time for sex!*
- *Jean Pierre Rampal (Bach flute concertos)*
- *Great place to have sex*
- *Bowl made in Wednesday night pottery class*
- *Latest Anne Lamott novel*
- *Masterworks of French Impressionists*

HERE'S HOW YOU SEE YOUR LIVING ROOM NOW THAT YOU ARE A MOM

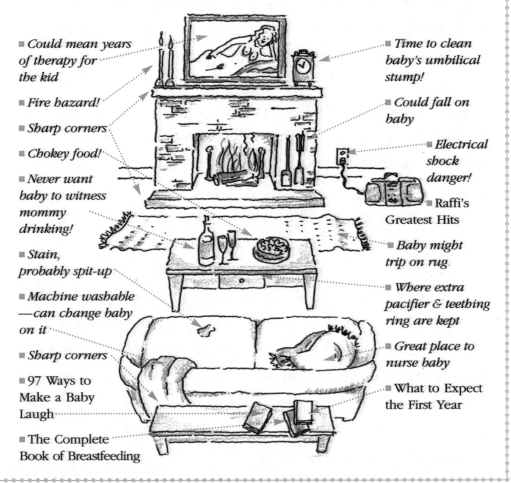

■ *Could mean years of therapy for the kid*

■ *Fire hazard!*

■ *Sharp corners*

■ *Chokey food!*

■ *Never want baby to witness mommy drinking!*

■ *Stain, probably spit-up*

■ *Machine washable —can change baby on it*

■ *Sharp corners*

■ 97 Ways to Make a Baby Laugh

■ The Complete Book of Breastfeeding

■ *Time to clean baby's umbilical stump!*

■ *Could fall on baby*

■ *Electrical shock danger!*

■ Raffi's Greatest Hits

■ *Baby might trip on rug*

■ *Where extra pacifier & teething ring are kept*

■ *Great place to nurse baby*

■ What to Expect the First Year

TROMPE L'OEIL TIDINESS

As a new mom, you are in Housework Survival Mode. You are not looking to meet Mrs. Cleaver's standards—or even the Beav's, for that matter. You just want to be able to locate the refrigerator and have a place to change the baby's diaper.

But just about the time you've convinced yourself that you can lower your standards dramatically without anyone suffering any permanent damage, you realize that this is the time when *everyone you've ever known* wants to stop in and make a fuss over the baby.

Despite the fact that babies fall into the "If you've seen one, you've seen them all" category (see page 18), people are making the pilgrimage to see yours. So the house needs to be picked up enough so it will not be a horrifying distraction. Here's a tip: Don't even try for clean—just aim for the General Impression of Relative Tidiness. Here's how it works, based on a hypothetical visitor situation:

4:56 Your pals from work call. They have a present for the baby and want to stop by in a few minutes on their way home. Because they are bringing a gift (probably a nice big one because they all chipped in on it), you agree to allow them to come for a visit.

4:57 Develop a plan of action. Determine which door you will let your guests in and along what route you will lead them into which room. You will only clean along the Designated Route (D.R.).

4:58 Put the baby gate across the stairs leading to the second floor. Only babies can unlock baby gates, and we can presume that your co-workers, coming straight from work, are baby-free.

4:59 Walk the D.R., throwing away anything that would be universally recognized as garbage, including, but not limited to, newspapers from two months ago, apple cores, deflated "Congratulations" balloons, and the like.

5:00 Again walking only along the D.R., take every item that you would label "clutter" and hide it in one of these underutilized temporary storage spots: the oven, the dryer, or the washing machine. You can opt for the more traditional under-the-sofa or behind-the-easy-chair storage spots, but if anyone suspects you of conducting a Quick Clean, those are the first places they'll look.

5:03 Dust only the coffee table. Then place some candy, nuts, Diet Cokes, and a bottle of wine there to focus your guests' attention on the snacks and away from cobwebby corners.

5:05 Tuck fabric softener sheets in-between sofa cushions and behind pillows for the impression of freshness.

5:07 Put the dog in the kitchen (and if you don't have a dog, holler for the neighbor's) and have him eat the stuff off the floor. He can also lick any plates before they go into the dishwasher.

5:08 Fill the sink with super-sudsy water and throw anything in there that won't dissolve within the next 45 minutes or so.

5:10 Make a couple of sweeps with the vacuum cleaner across the middle of the floor in each room (along the D.R.) to make those

nice vacuum lines, giving the general impression that vacuuming has indeed occurred.

5:13 Remove a few lightbulbs, unplug a couple of lamps, and close the drapes. *Remember: dark and dim are preferable to dirty.*

5:14 Get ready to open the predetermined door and usher your guests along the Designated Route!

Note: All you need to do to yourself is run a comb through your hair. When you were pregnant, people came to see you. Now that you are a mother, they come to see the baby. That's just the way that one goes.

New Mom Faux Pas

No. 2

NOT KNOWING
WHAT IS A UNIVERSAL BABY
ISSUE AND WHAT IS A PERSONAL
QUIRK OF YOUR BABY'S

BABYPROOFING

The widely accepted concept of babyproofing is all wrong. The goal should be to protect the *house* from the *baby,* not vice versa. Here's what may happen if you do not protect your house:

1. Baby will take graham cracker (1a) and jam it into VCR (1b), thus rendering VCR unusable.

2. Baby will flush all magnetic alphabet letters other than Q, Z, V, and J (2a) down the toilet (2b), making it impossible to spell anything meaningful as well as causing the toilet to overflow.

3. Baby will stuff cat (3a) into hamper (3b), where freaked-out kitty will throw up on fine washables.

4. Baby will fill tub (4) with water and drop in the following items to see if they float: your husband's 1896 pocket watch (will not float), photos of your grandmother as a baby (will float initially), your Palm Pilot (nope), one of your diamond earrings (uh-uh), and a paper cup (yes!).

5. Baby will play with TV remote (5), resulting in the selection of 47 Pay-per-View movies.

6. Baby will take your nine bottles of perfume (6a), pour them into your husband's cowboy hat from his Montana boyhood (6b), and then dump it all into your sweater drawer (6c).

7. Baby will remove diaper in front of refrigerator (7a), then proceed to poop in your saucepan (7b), on the leather recliner (7c), and under your authentic Oriental rug (7d), where it will remain undiscovered for three days.

8. Baby will take your car keys (8a) and scratch this familiar baby mark: 〰 on the antique walnut coffee table (8b) before tossing them in the air, after which they land in the garbage disposal (8c).

9. Baby will tear pages out of book of Impressionist Art (9a) and use vaseline from diaper bag (9b) to stick them to living room wall (9c).

THE CAR

Remember analogies from the SATs? Here's a Mommy Analogy for you:

Driving alone IS TO *driving with your baby*

as

Pedaling a Big Wheel IS TO _____.

1. piloting *Air Force One*

2. racing in the Indy 500

3. being at the controls of a nuclear submarine

CORRECT ANSWER: All of the above, simultaneously.

HOW A TWO-MILE TRIP CAN TAKE TWO HOURS

1 **10:00 A.M.** Leave home for 10:15 pediatrician appointment.

2 **10:06 A.M.** Pull over to make sure you remembered to put baby in car (the curse of the backseat, rear-facing car seat).

3 **10:09 A.M.** Pull over again to make sure you buckled in baby's car seat.

4 **10:11 A.M.** Return to house because you forgot diaper bag.

5 **10:17 A.M.** Pull over because you think the sun is in the baby's eyes.

6 **10:25 A.M.** Return to house again because you discover in doctor's parking lot that you forgot list of questions for pediatrician that you spent many days compiling.

7 **10:30 A.M.** Call on cell phone to tell doctor's receptionist that you

are running a little late.

8   **10:40 A.M.** Pull over because baby wants to nurse.

9   **11:08 A.M.** Return to house because baby spit up and both of you need a change of clothes.

10   **11:25 A.M.** Pull over to make sure you remembered to put baby in car this time; return to house because baby is wearing only one shoe.

11   **11:38 A.M.** Pull over because baby is making weird choking noises. (Add to list of questions for pediatrician.)

12   **11:46 A.M.** Pull over because now baby isn't making any noise at all.

13   **12:00 P.M.** Arrive at pediatrician's office one hour and 45 minutes late, just as the office closes for lunch.

10 AMAZING THINGS MOMS CAN DO WHILE DRIVING

1. Hold bottle for baby

2. Find something baby dropped

3. Put hat on/take hat off

4. Take shoe off/put shoe back on

5. Create shade for baby

6. Pump breasts

7. Pick off Cheerio stuck to baby's thumb

8. Sing (with hand motions) "Do Your Ears Hang Low?" to keep baby from falling asleep

9. Pump brakes and rock car from side to side to create illusion of movement while car is stopped at traffic light to keep baby from waking up

10. And, when utterly desperate, nurse baby

HOW TO PEE WHILE DRIVING

"*The strangest thing I ever did while driving with my baby in the car was pee. I'd had two cups of coffee before I got in the car to drive to the airport—big mistake. About a half hour into the trip, the baby had fallen asleep and I had to pee so badly I was in agony, but I also didn't want to pull over to use a rest room because I would have had to wake the baby up. So I grabbed one of his diapers and stuck it under me and peed in it while I was cruising at about 55 mph. Thankfully, Pampers are as absorbent as they say they are.*" —LISA

GROCERY SHOPPING WITH THE BABY

THE PLAN

At 11 A.M., you and the baby will drive to the grocery store, where you will select the items on your list, pay for them, bag them, and return home by noon to put them away.

THE REALITY

9:08 A.M. Examine meager contents of pantry and refrigerator.

9:24 A.M. Write extensive grocery list with the plucky optimism of a new mother who has not yet attempted to grocery shop with her baby.

9:38 A.M. Feed baby.

10:01 A.M. Change baby's diaper.

10:05 A.M. Attempt to put baby down for a nap so that she will not be cranky in the store. She senses the urgency of your attempt, and does the now-familiar stiffen-and-screech when you put her down.

10:34 A.M. Give her a bath, rediaper,

and rock her while humming the entire *Lullabies for Newborns* CD. Try the nap again. No go.

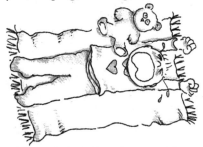

10:56 A.M. Abandon the nap idea altogether, and dress baby in the Baby Gap outfit with the matching vest, hat, and booties.

11:08 A.M. Baby projectile-poops in

Baby Gap outfit, rendering it permanently unwearable.

11:16 A.M. Change baby into equally cute and complicated Baby Dior outfit. Baby finishes projectile pooping.

11:26 A.M. Change baby into T-shirt and diaper.

11:39 A.M. Put baby in car seat. Check diaper bag for essentials. (Realize that diaper bag, though only slightly smaller than steamer trunks used by passengers on the *Titanic,* does not contain any diapers. Mentally add diapers to grocery list.)

11:52 A.M. Drive 0.3 mile to grocery store.

11:57 A.M. Arrive at grocery store. Baby is asleep.

12:03 P.M. Return home. As if handling a live grenade, carefully transfer baby from car seat to crib.

12:07 P.M. Baby wakes up wailing as you tiptoe out of the room, proving what every mother comes to know—half a nap is worse than none.

12:14 P.M. Put wailing baby back in car seat.

12:28 P.M. Return to grocery store.

12:35 P.M. Carry cranky baby inside only to discover that the carts with the built-in baby seats are all taken. Return to car to get car seat for baby to sit in, which takes up virtually all the room in the grocery cart.

12:42 P.M. Begin in produce aisle, where baby, who is pulling her own hair, moves from cranky ("eh-eh-eh") to downright miserable ("AAAAAAAHHHH!").

12:53 P.M. Make quick detour to baby aisle and "borrow" plastic telephone toy for baby to suck on.

12:59 P.M. Return to produce aisle. Look through pockets for grocery list. Realize that list is on kitchen counter. Try to reconstruct list as baby repeatedly bangs herself on the head with plastic phone and winds up for another screech.

1:08 P.M. Assume that potatoes, generally agreed upon as a food staple, are on the list. Ditto apples.

Is it a little BOY?

1:17 P.M. Old lady from church who always calls you "Allison" stops you to fuss over fussy baby. Gives well-intended 1920s advice about what might be wrong as baby continues to wail.

1:24 P.M. Ditch old lady and head for the snacks, where you hand baby a crinkly bag of chips to maul and suck and throw a few bags of pretzels into the cart because stress makes you crave salt. Leave drooly baby phone in snack aisle.

1:39 P.M. Hear your name called over loudspeaker as you are heading to frozen foods.

1:43 P.M. Cross store (2.3-mile trip) to customer-service desk to find

that deli supervisor has a name that sounds (especially with baby screeching in the background) remarkably like yours.

1:51 P.M. Momentarily consider abandoning grocery cart and aborting grocery mission. Reconsider because stomach is growling and head for paper-goods aisle, grabbing a loaf of bread along the way. Leave mauled bag of chips among breads.

2:02 P.M. Discover that rocking cart back and forth as you push it at about 27 miles an hour seems to calm baby. Just as baby begins to wind down, retired neighbor with nothing on today's to-do list but grocery shopping stops your cart so he can look at baby and make unwelcome comments about the baby's name.

2:17 P.M. Grab carton of milk in dairy section. Baby is momentarily distracted by balloons bobbing near the cake counter and stops crying.

2:25 P.M. As you leave dairy, baby can no longer see balloons and commences screeching. You quickly return to cake counter and negotiate purchase of balloons.

2:31 P.M. Head for checkout line.

2:38 P.M. Put items on conveyor belt and force a laugh at cashier's lame joke about babies being on sale today.

2:40 P.M. Look for bank card as cashier gives you the total. Realize with horror that bank card is in pocketbook that is on kitchen counter next to grocery list.

2:43 P.M. Frantically empty contents of pockets onto conveyor belt. Pockets contain one dried-up baby wipe, a sunflower seed, a piece of Wrigley's gum and $14.22. Decide which items totaling less than $14.22 you cannot live without. You choose milk, apples, Diet Coke, and pretzels.

2:45 P.M. Refuse offer from complete stranger who wants to pick up howling balloon-less baby as you bag your four items.

2:51 P.M. Put groceries in back of car and realize you forgot diapers.

But you didn't have enough money to pay for them anyway.

2:55 P.M. Put still-howling baby into car.

3:04 P.M. Drive home. Baby falls asleep.

3:14 P.M. Carefully transfer baby to crib.

3:17 P.M. Tiptoe out of room; baby wakes up screaming.

3:24 P.M. Feed and rock baby in an attempt to recapture the nap.

3:47 P.M. Milk, still in back of car, begins to spoil.

4:28 P.M. Baby finally falls asleep. You decide to put her into the crib.

4:29 P.M. As soon as you stop rocking, baby wakes up and starts crying.

4:30 P.M. You put crying baby into crib anyway and go downstairs where you sit in the kitchen and listen to baby crying on baby monitor.

4:45 P.M. Husband arrives home to find you sitting at the table listening to baby crying and asks you what's for dinner.

THE STONE SOUP PHENOMENON

Here's the good news. . . . You *can* make dinner with the paltry assortment of stuff you have in your fridge! Here's how.

RECIPES

LA VIANDE DÉLICIEUSE

Mix about 6 oz. of mustard and 10 oz. of jelly over low heat. Slice up the package of hot dogs, add them to mustard/jelly, and heat through. (Refrigerate leftovers for tomorrow's lunch!)

LA POMME DE TERRE SUCCULENTE

Cut the potatoes into slices. Put them in a plastic bag with some Italian dressing. Shake the bag. Arrange the potatoes on a broiler pan and broil for about 10 to 15 minutes, turning once.

LES LÉGUMES ALLÉCHANTS

Beat the 2 eggs, a cup of the beer, and 1¼ cups of the flour. Dip broccoli and carrots (and any other veggies that may be hiding in the crisper) in the batter and fry.

TA-DA! DINNER!

Note: By making up a French name for each of these dishes, you add a certain *je-ne-sais-quoi* elegance to the meal. It doesn't really matter what the French name means (unless, of course, your dinner companions are French).

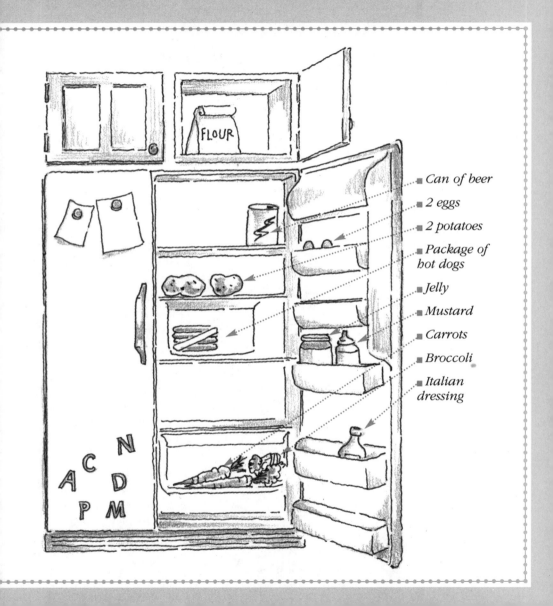

- Can of beer
- 2 eggs
- 2 potatoes
- Package of hot dogs
- Jelly
- Mustard
- Carrots
- Broccoli
- Italian dressing

FLOUR

"CAN I HOLD YOUR BABY . . . ?"

Because your baby is the world's cutest, everybody, including complete strangers, will want to hold him. Not everyone is a suitable candidate. Here's what to look out for.

WOULD-BE BABY HOLDER CHECKLIST

☐ I have washed my hands with antibacterial soap and scrubbed my nails with a nailbrush.

☐ I have changed into sterile cotton clothing.

☐ I have a doctor's note stating that I am free of contagious diseases.

☐ I have donned a surgeon's mask.

☐ I have passed a Breathalyzer test.

☐ I am sitting in a sturdy chair, waiting for the baby to be handed to me.

■ *Hair doohickey could poke baby*

■ *Poor vision: might trip and drop baby*

■ *Earring: choking hazard if it falls out and lands in baby's mouth*

■ *Red nose: might have been nipping at the cooking sherry*

■ *Will kiss baby and leave big red lip print*

■ *Large bosom: could smother baby*

■ *Slip is showing: not sure what this fashion faux pas means for your baby, but it can't be a good thing*

■ *"Trippy" heels*

BABY HOLDER CANDIDATE'S QUIZ

You must answer all of the questions below correctly (as determined by the individual mother) to be considered as a baby holder. You have 15 minutes to complete these questions. Please use a no. 2 pencil. Neatness and spelling do count.

1. Are there any circumstances in which throwing the baby up in the air (and catching him) are acceptable? If so, what are they?

....

....

2. Would you pass the baby to another person (other than the mother or father) without first obtaining permission? If so, please explain.

....

....

3. If the baby spits up while you are holding her, will you want to return her to her mother? What if she projectile vomits?

....

....

4. What is your rocking speed, on a scale of 1 to 10, with 1 being very slow and 10 being very fast? (Circle one.)

1 2 3 4 5 6 7 8 9 10

5. Are you a *(1)* baby back rubber or *(2)* baby back patter? (Circle one.)

6. If the baby falls asleep while you are holding her, will you continue to hold her or put her down? Why? Will excessive drooling while sleeping impact your decision?

....

....

....

7. If the baby's diaper needs changing while you are holding her, will you find her mother or change her yourself? Will it make a difference whether it is #1 or #2?

....

....

....

8. Do you consider yourself to be a clumsy person? (Circle one.)

Yes   No

9. How many items have you dropped in the last week? (Circle one.)

0 1 2 3 4 5 more than 5

Bonus Essay Question: What are the six basic newborn reflexes and what is the relevance of each to your anticipated interaction with the baby? (Please use a separate piece of paper for your answer.)

12 THINGS YOU CAN DO DURING THOSE 10-MINUTE CATNAPS YOUR BABY TAKES INSTEAD OF THE DECENT 2-HOUR NAPS EVERYONE ELSE'S BABY SEEMS TO TAKE

You can accomplish quite a bit during those quickie dozes your baby takes during the day. The big question is: Do you *want* to accomplish things, or do you want to enjoy yourself? After all, you are justifiably tired and cranky and deserve to do something that will make you happy, not some old boring chore.

Following is a list of 12 things that you probably need to do, each with a related suggestion of something more fun that you can do instead.

ONE

You should clean the stuff out of your refrigerator that expired last month.

INSTEAD: Treat yourself to sour cream-and-onion potato chips, followed by chocolate-chip cookies (so that you end on sweet).

TWO

You should make your bed.

INSTEAD: Flop onto your unmade bed, close your eyes, and fantasize about your incredibly good-looking dentist.

THREE

You should replace some of the lightbulbs that have burned out (or those you removed to create the "dim" effect for visitors—see page 158).

INSTEAD: Go outside where it's nice and bright and lie in the sun.

FOUR

You should hand wash some sweaters.

INSTEAD: Order three new sweaters from the L. L. Bean Catalog.

FIVE

You should pay the phone bill.

INSTEAD: Call your best friend from high school who now lives in Seattle.

SIX

You should put the baby photos in the baby-photo album.

INSTEAD: Look through your old photo albums and remember how you thought you were fat back in those days when really you weren't fat at all, relatively speaking.

SEVEN

You should sort through your old *Redbook* magazines and throw away all of the really old ones.

INSTEAD: Put your feet up and reread all of the "Most Embarrassing Moments" sections.

EIGHT

You should organize the junk drawer in your kitchen.

INSTEAD: Open the drawer and make an interesting sculpture with the 43 baggie ties that are in there.

NINE

You should make a grocery list.

INSTEAD: Make a list of all of the reasons your husband should be extremely grateful to be married to you.

TEN

You should do 10 minutes of sit-ups.

INSTEAD: You just sit up and watch 10 minutes of C-Span.

ELEVEN

You should go through the baby's clothes and take out the ones that are too small.

INSTEAD: Go on the Internet and order yourself a pair of expensive jeans two sizes too small in order to force yourself to lose weight.

TWELVE

You should match socks.

INSTEAD: Turn the white socks into a family of hand puppets you will use to amuse the baby when she wakes up.

BEFORE-BABY POCKETBOOK

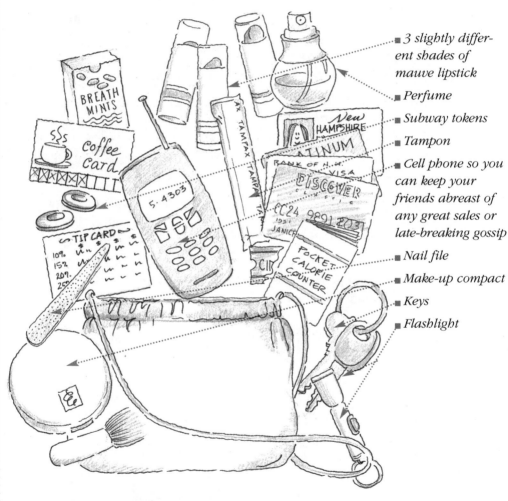

- *3 slightly different shades of mauve lipstick*
- *Perfume*
- *Subway tokens*
- *Tampon*
- *Cell phone so you can keep your friends abreast of any great sales or late-breaking gossip*
- *Nail file*
- *Make-up compact*
- *Keys*
- *Flashlight*

AFTER-BABY POCKETBOOK

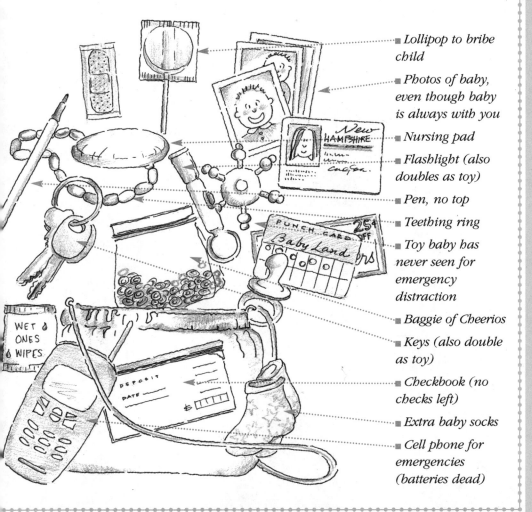

- Lollipop to bribe child
- Photos of baby, even though baby is always with you
- Nursing pad
- Flashlight (also doubles as toy)
- Pen, no top
- Teething ring
- Toy baby has never seen for emergency distraction
- Baggie of Cheerios
- Keys (also double as toy)
- Checkbook (no checks left)
- Extra baby socks
- Cell phone for emergencies (batteries dead)

BABY MAKES THREE

The transition from couplehood to parenthood is a roller-coaster ride with more ups and downs, twists and turns, than the Cyclone. Once you and your guy have bought those tickets to ride, you have two basic options: You can throw your hands up in the air and try to convince yourselves you're having fun, or you can cling to the safety bar in terror  and wonder how you got yourselves into this predicament. I recommend the first option.

New parenthood is a challenging time because never are the differences between men and women more obvious than when they are raising a child together. A dad's idea of when a diaper needs to be changed, what constitutes a healthy lunch, and whether there are any lasting effects of watching professional wrestling on television is usually radically different from a mom's. A dad may fluctuate between wanting to be a better mother than you are and wanting to be a baby himself. And while his libido is still pegged at 10, yours has bottomed out in the negative numbers.

But never fear: Like all roller-coaster rides, this one, too, will come to an end (even though you'll be in the amusement park for a while longer). Once you step off, you can decide whether or not you want to buy a ticket to the Baby Number Two Roller-Coaster Ride. (Note: It's never quite as scary the second time around.)

"HELPFUL" DADS

THE THINGS NEW DADS DO THAT DRIVE NEW MOMS CRAZY

"*He'll offer to take the baby so that I can get some chores done, but then he follows me around the house with the baby, saying to him, 'Where's Mommy? Do you see Mommy?'*"

"*After I've been up several nights in a row with the baby, my husband may offer to get up with her. But as soon as she starts crying, I wake him up and he'll mumble, 'I'm gonna wait and see if she just cries it out' and then he promptly falls back to sleep.*"

"*He thinks that if he asks me 27 questions when he's feeding the baby that I won't ask him to do it again.*"

"*He won't use ointment on our son's bottom when he's changing him because he thinks it's 'girly.'*"

"*He'll feed the baby when I'm gone, but he'll leave a sink full of dirty dishes behind. I mean, you feed a baby applesauce and carrots and you create eight dirty dishes?*"

"*He feels triumphant if he can get the baby to eat or drink weird things she's never had before. One time I came home from the grocery store and he was giving her olive juice.*"

"*When he changes the baby's diaper, he uses half a box of wipes.*"

"*In the midst of total baby bedlam, with the twins crawling around crying, torturing each other as well as the dog, he will sit on the sofa and read the newspaper as if he were all alone.*"

"*He gets the baby all riled up just before bedtime and then hands me this overtired, hyper basketcase to try to put to sleep.*"

"*He never actually throws away the dirty diaper and inevitably the dog finds it and thinks it's a doggy toy.*"

"*If the baby is fussy, he'll make the general comment 'The baby is crying,' as if he could not possibly be part of the solution.*"

"*When he returns home with the baby, no matter where they've been or how long they've been gone, she's missing one of her little socks or booties. And we are talking every time he takes her out.*"

"*I'll come home at lunchtime and find him sitting there eating a huge meal while* the baby is fussing in her high chair waiting to be fed. It's *always* his *stomach first!*"

"*H*e can't stand to see the baby playing contentedly. He has to stir the pot. He comes over to her, tweaks her cheeks, messes up her hair, tickles her, and as soon as she starts fussing, he leaves."

"*H*e will put the baby in his Exer-saucer in the yard, go into the garage to get something, and—I swear!—completely forget the baby's out there! An hour later, the baby's still sitting in the middle of the lawn all alone and my husband is fiddling around at his workbench."

"*H*e will get up with the baby at night sometimes, but he doesn't seem to understand that you need to keep her in 'nighttime mode' as much as possible. He turns on the light in her room, greets her heartily, and starts playing games with her!"

"*I* will get all four kids completely dressed in matching outfits for portraits or church or some family event, and inevitably my husband will decide to feed the twins sweet potatoes or beets or some super-staining baby food. He just doesn't seem to think things all the way through."

NOTES FOR DADDY

Do you ever wonder what *really* happens when you leave your husband and the baby alone with a list of how the day should go? Do you actually believe that he puts on the *Mozart for Babies* CD and takes out the number flashcards right after feeding the baby spinach and plums for lunch? Does he air-dry her bottom for five minutes so she won't get a rash and remember to turn off the phone and put notes on all of the doors when she goes down for a nap?

Not likely...

Mom's Notes

Honey, if Ava seems sad today, tell her "Mommy loves you and she will be back at 5:30 tonight." Show her the clock and point out where the big hand and little hand will be at 5:30. (We've been working on time this week.)

Here is Ava's schedule for the day:

11:00 – Play French language tape (we're up to tape 3, side 2) while Ava is in her jumpy seat. (Remember that article we read about introducing a second language as early as possible?)

12:15 – Feed Ava her lunch in this order: peas, bananas, 2 ounces of bow-tie pasta. Rinse her dishes in HOT water and then wipe dry.

12:30 – Change Ava's diaper. (Be sure to warm the wipes ahead of time.) Her bottom should be air-dried. Don't forget the diaper-rash cream.

Dad's Notes

Not necessary– She didn't seem to notice you were gone.

Neg on the tapes. She was happy sucking on her toes while I checked the score of the game.

Did you know she likes this stuff raw (like, crunchy?)??

The dog can lick them cleaner than I can wash them. I mean, I'm just guessing he could.

12:45 – Ava can play with the toys I showed you yesterday that are designed to stimulate left-brain activity. They are in her basket of toys in the family room. She also likes her farm-animal flashcards (you need to say the sound each animal makes as you show her the card).

1:00 – Put Ava in stroller with plastic cup of Cheerios. She should wear her pink shoes and her ducky sun hat (NOT the rainbow sun hat). Diaper bag is already packed with the following: lightweight throw, pacifier, extra diapers and wipes, juice bottle, teething ring, squeaky porcupine, doll with blue dress, and farm-animal board book.

Walk to playground and park the stroller near the slide because she likes to watch the children playing. (Be sure she is not facing the sun!)

1:50 – Leave playground. (Do not let her fall asleep on the way home!)

2:00 – Give Ava her prenap bath (see attached sheet for bathing steps) and massage. Put on a clean diaper and dress her in comfy napping clothes. Put pink blanket in the dryer so it is

Actually, she was a little bit lost during this very short time period.... I mean, you didn't tell me she could ROLL. Found her under the couch (NO, she was NOT crying, just a little tiny bit stunned).

Couldn't find these. But she likes playing with the toilet plunger (YES, I washed it off before I let her suck on it !!)

OK, I DID put her in the stroller, but then we decided that it was a little TOO SUNNY to go out so we parked the stroller in the TV room to wait for the sun to go in a little.

Don't know what these are anyway.

warm when you put it on her. Dim lights, play Mozart CD on volume level 2, rock her for 15 minutes while she drinks bottle (premade in fridge; heat in pan of water on stove with top removed until lukewarm; test on wrist). She will also need her pacifier, her extra pacifier, bunny-bun, and Mother Goose in her crib. Close the door halfway and make sure the baby monitor is on, volume level 8.

3:15 – Check to make sure she hasn't kicked blanket off.

4:30 – Wake her up so that she will go back to sleep at 7:30. Awaken with same routine used to put her to sleep, only in reverse.

4:35 – Feed her a snack of toast cut into farm animal shapes (cookie cutters are next to toaster) and apple juice diluted 2:1.

5:00 – Read aloud from *Poems for Wee Ones*. We're on page 34.

Numbers for poison control, the pediatrician, Kathy across the street (who is also a nurse), and my mother are by the phone. Have fun!

She fell asleep in front of the TV, so I didn't get to do this stuff

Or this stuff.

She woke up with 2 minutes to play in the fourth quarter

Couldn't find the bread. Made a substitution: Cheez Doodles

We both thought this was boring, so we looked through your Victoria's Secret Catalog. (We both liked the bra and panties set on page 21)

Not sure you want to leave us alone EVERY Saturday... I think the baby REALLY missed you.

"WHY I WANT TO BE THE BABY."

by Daddy

SEXCUSES...

THE FIVE BEST WAYS NEW MOMS CAN AVOID SEX

Unless you're like my Aunt Betty (now there's a long story), you won't want to avoid sex for the rest of your life. But right now, after the tearing and stretching and ripping and bleeding and subsequent sleepless night after sleepless night . . . well, it's no wonder you are not feeling particularly hot 'n' horny. Think of your temporary disinterest as Mother Nature's way of keeping you from adding to your flock in another nine months.

Other than an outright refusal when your husband puts the moves on (which a few of my friends insist is the only way), there are subtle things you can say and do to postpone the "fun":

1. Use the distraction or redirection technique. This is a skill you will need when you have a toddler anyway, so you might as well learn it now. Rent a Clint Eastwood movie, leave a *Sports Illustrated* magazine or a tool catalog on his pillow—anything to take his mind off of "it."

2. Use lots of scary female medical terminology when talking about sex and the area "down under." Avoid any cutesy little nicknames the two of you invented. Instead, get clinical. Discuss your "sutures in the perinatal region."

3. Borrow one of his mother's nightgowns and tell him that he should call you "Mommy" now that you are one.

4. As soon as the two of you get into bed, start listing the bills that came in the mail that day. If none came, make some up. The thought of paying bills is a real mood killer for most guys.

5. After the baby has been up for three nights in a row, say that you can't wait to make another one. *He'll* start avoiding *you.*

Note: If none of these subtle techniques works, put the baby to sleep between you.

WHAT'S HE THINKING?

Ｈow well do you know your husband? Take this quiz to see if you can tell what the new daddy is thinking in each scenario.

IS HE . . .

a. Mentally comparing the nutritional value of formula versus breast milk?

b. Wondering if he should offer to bring you a glass of water (remembering that nursing makes you thirsty)?

c. Peeved because he does not like to share his toys?

IS HE . . .

a. Thinking about covering the baby with an extra blanket because the room feels a little chilly?

b. Wondering if he should wake the baby soon so that he will go to bed at a reasonable time tonight?

c. Calculating the odds of the baby waking up if he tries out his new circular saw in the garage?

IS HE . . .

a. Wondering if it's possible to potty train a baby who can't sit up yet?

b. Estimating what the lady next door would charge him to change the baby's diaper?

c. Contemplating the likelihood that you will believe the baby *just* pooped as you were walking in the door?

A NIGHT AWAY
FROM BABY

Now that you are parents, an evening out on the town is anything but a relaxing date. Oh, your husband still sees the world in pretty much the same way he did before he became a dad (see page 196).

You, however, see everything through the hyperfocused eyes of a new mom (see page 197)— and not just when you are with the baby, but every single minute of every single day, including special "couple time." That makes it more than a little challenging to leave your cares behind and paint the town red with your man.

SECONDARY SLEEP DEPRIVATION??

"Some friends from my office stopped by to see the baby last week. My husband Steven started complaining to them about how wiped out he is because it disturbs his sleep when I get up at night to feed the baby!"

—MARISSA

MOMMY/WIFE TIME LINE

You're so tempted to put your baby first—he's so sweet and helpless and his breath is always fresh. And hey—your husband's a big boy: He can take care of himself. But when you look to the future, you may want to rethink your policy of Baby First, All the Time, Every

	1ST YEAR	2ND YEAR	3RD YEAR	4TH YEAR	5TH YEAR	6TH YEAR	7TH YEAR	8TH YEAR	9TH YEAR	10TH YEAR
THE BABY	Smiles every time he sees you and cries when you leave the room Says his first word: "Mama"	Loves to sit on your lap and read *Are You My Mother?*	Wants to marry you when he grows up	Has developed bad habit of wiping his nose on your pants	Insists on wearing Spiderman outfit to kindergarten every day	Won't let you kiss him at the bus stop	Begs for (and gets) puppy	Is tired of puppy (now dog) Will only talk about baseball	Thinks girls, homework, and vegetables are all stupid	Loses an average of one sweatshirt and one pair of sneakers every week
THE HUSBAND	Wants to breast-feed like the baby Changing diapers makes him sick to his stomach	Baby bumps his head when husband is supposed to be watching him	Teaches baby Three Stooges eye poke	Wants to cuddle with you after you've had a bad day	Will listen to you complain about your boss every night	Expands cooking skills beyond "grilling" so he can make dinner the other 10 months of the year	Will gladly turn off the baseball game to make out with you	Takes over puppy duties	Watches *Sex and the City* with you	Occasionally leaves 'sticky' love notes for you on bathroom mirror

The row label for the year row reads: YEARS OF MOTHERHOOD

Time. Sweet newborns turn into cranky two-year-olds who become close-to-intolerable 13-year-olds. But your husband will always be the same good guy who thinks you have a cute butt and makes the world's best lasagne.

Here's a typical 20-year scenario:

THE BABY									
Will only talk about soccer	Thinks his friends are cool and you are dorky	Won't leave his room because he has pimples	Drives friend's motorbike through high school cafeteria on a dare	Allows motorbike friend to tatoo rattlesnake on his ankle	Wants to quit school to become a magician's apprentice	Needs to borrow $4,500 for a "once-in-a-lifetime opportunity"	Stops by the house just to shower and change	Wants to move in with girlfriend who is 4 years older than he is	Wants to move back home with girlfriend because magician gig isn't panning out

11TH YEAR	12TH YEAR	13TH YEAR	14TH YEAR	15TH YEAR	16TH YEAR	17TH YEAR	18TH YEAR	19TH YEAR	20TH YEAR
Is willing to spend his whole vacation with your parents	Worries about you when you have to drive in bad weather	Still thinks you're hot, especially wen you wear your cut-offs	Washes and vacuums out your car when you are harried	Encourages you to go back to school to get your Master's	Buys you a sexy sports car for your birthday	Reads the same novel you are reading for Book Club so he can discuss it with you	Rearranges work schedule so he can cheer you on in the tennis finals at the club	Waits up for you after your Investment Club meetings	On your 20th anniversary, says he'd marry you all over again

THE HUSBAND

OF GRANDPARENTS & GODPARENTS

GRANDMA AND GRAMPS

The good news: They have lots of free time and want to help. The bad news: They have lots of free time and want to help. They're wonderful people, really, and they do mean well and they never do anything *horribly* wrong, like giving the baby a machete to play with, but it's the little things. And over time, the little things add up to one gigantic, immensely annoying thing.

Because misery loves company, allow me to share some stories from other frustrated moms.

Generic baby products she thinks are as good as the brands you buy

Parenting books with notes marking what you do wrong

30-year-old hand-me-downs

PENELOPE LEACH'S COMPETITION

"*My* mother-in-law has lots of advice to give—of course it's all from 1953–1957. She was convinced that if we taped a quarter to Alex's belly button, it would turn his outie into an innie."

—CLAIRE

A CLOSE SHAVE

"*My* mother-in-law decided to 'surprise' me and give our son his first haircut. She planned on giving him a buzz cut the way she used to for my husband when he was little, but she didn't realize that the electric razor was set for a close shave. Of course the first swipe she made was right down the middle of his head. He had an anti-Mohawk."

—IRENE

BETTER VISIT THE SOUTHWEST ASAP

"*My* in-laws think it's ridiculous that I use cloth diapers when disposables are so convenient. I try to patiently explain my reasons, but my father-in-law comes back with, 'When the landfills get filled up, they can start throwing garbage into the Grand Canyon.' How do you respond to that?"

—MAY

JUNK-FOOD GRANNY

"*It's* as if my mother-in-law makes a real effort to find the worst food she possibly could to feed the baby. Like for breakfast, she'll break frosted Pop Tarts into little pieces for him and give him Kool-Aid to drink."

—KRISTEN

HELP!

"*My mother-in-law decides for herself how she can be 'helpful.' The other day, she came by and whisked the baby off for a 'quick' walk in the park. A good hour and a half later, my friend arrived with her baby for a prearranged play date. I had to go out searching for my mother-in-law to retrieve my son.*"

—KARYN

DAIRY QUEEN

"*My mother-in-law doesn't believe my son is lactose intolerant. She thinks the concept is silly— that he can be conditioned to digest dairy products. She will feed him ice cream and cheese on the sly just to prove she's right.*"

—LUCY

LAVISH AND THOUGHTFUL GIFT-GIVER

"*When my daughter was born, my mother-in-law got her an outfit: She bought it from the dollar store and it was supposed to be for a Cabbage Patch doll!*"

—KERRI

NANA SPEAK

TRANSLATING WHAT GRANDMA SAYS

Having your mother-in-law visit is akin to hosting a foreign visitor. You may *think* you understand what she is saying, but chances are you're mistaken. Here's a guide to help you out:

WHAT SHE SAYS: *"Do you think the baby needs a sweater?"*

WHAT SHE MEANS: *"Put a sweater on the baby."*

WHAT SHE SAYS: *"I find it just amazing that she gets enough milk through nursing alone!"*

WHAT SHE MEANS: *"She's not getting enough milk. The poor thing is starving to death."*

WHAT SHE SAYS: *"You look tired."*

WHAT SHE MEANS: *"Don't drop my grandson."*

WHAT SHE SAYS: *"That's an interesting way to burp the baby."*

WHAT SHE MEANS: *"That's a stupid way to burp the baby."*

WHAT SHE SAYS: *"Can we stop by for a few minutes?"*

WHAT SHE MEANS: *"Can we stop by for 6 hours?"*

WHAT SHE SAYS: *"Where did you come up with the baby's name?"*

WHAT SHE MEANS: *"Why didn't you name the baby after his grandfather?"*

WHAT SHE SAYS: *"Don't worry about picking up the house for us, dear."*

WHAT SHE MEANS: *"I can't believe my son married such a slob."*

WHAT SHE SAYS: *"Did you lay out this little bunny sweater for him to wear to the park today?"*

WHAT SHE MEANS: *"You're going to turn my grandson into a sissy."*

WHAT SHE SAYS: *"Why, I think she has your mother's hands."*

WHAT SHE MEANS: *"The poor thing got stuck with those weird, bony hands your mother has."*

WHAT SHE SAYS: *"How fancy: a battery-operated swing!"*

WHAT SHE MEANS: *"You can't rock the baby yourself? You need this contraption to do it for you?"*

WHAT SHE SAYS: *"Did you see this strange rash on her tummy?"*

WHAT SHE MEANS: *"I think her leg could fall off and it would take you a week to notice."*

WHAT SHE SAYS: *"Ooohhh… is this the quilt my sister made for the baby?"*

WHAT SHE MEANS: *"I know damn well this isn't the quilt my sister made. I just wanted to watch you squirm. What did you do, give it to Goodwill?? I could tell you didn't like it when she gave it to you."*

WHAT SHE SAYS: *"What would you like me to feed the baby while you're gone?"*

WHAT SHE MEANS: *"I'm going to feed the baby whatever I want to."*

WHAT SHE SAYS: *"Is the baby still sleeping in your bed?"*

WHAT SHE MEANS: *"You're going to roll over in the middle of the night and squish her."*

WHAT SHE SAYS: *"Do you think it's a little chilly in here, dear?"*

WHAT SHE MEANS: *"My grandson will catch pneumonia and die because you keep this house so cold."*

WHAT SHE SAYS: *"I see you're making your own baby food."*

WHAT SHE MEANS: *"What are you, a pioneer? Just go to the store and buy jars of squash like everybody else."*

WHAT SHE SAYS: *"Of course you need to do things your own way, dear."*

WHAT SHE MEANS: *"My way is better."*

KEEPING THINGS GRAND WITH THE GRANDPARENTS

REMEMBER THESE BEHAVIOR-MODIFICATION TIPS

One way to cope with overeager or out-of-control grandparents is to use the same behavior-modification techniques on them that you would use on a toddler. (And because you will soon have an actual toddler, these skills are very worth learning.)

If you are patient and consistent, you will begin to notice improvements in behavior. By the time your baby *is* a toddler, you will be able to take the grandparents *and* the toddler to the petting zoo without any of them acting out, having an uncontrollable tantrum, or crying because you don't want to bring home a goat.

ALLOW NATURAL CONSEQUENCES TO TEACH THE LESSON

WITH A TWO-YEAR-OLD: "See? The toy broke when you threw it. Now it won't work anymore."

WITH A GRANDPARENT: "See? The baby spit up all over when you twirled him around and blew raspberries on his stomach right after you gave him a bottle. Now we'll have to clean him up and feed him again."

MAKE SMALL CONCESSIONS

WITH A TWO-YEAR-OLD: "All right. You can push the stroller with bunny-bun in it until we get to the corner. But then *you* have to get in, too."

WITH A GRANDPARENT: "All right. You can go and look at the baby while she is napping. But then you have to back out of the room and let her sleep."

RELY HEAVILY ON POSITIVE REINFORCEMENT

WITH A TWO-YEAR-OLD: "I'm so glad to see you patting the dog instead of jamming your finger in his ear! I'll bet he'll want to play with you tomorrow, too!"

WITH A GRANDPARENT: "I'm so glad to see you reading him *Hop on Pop* instead of *Back Pain No More*! I'll bet he'll want to read with you tomorrow, too!"

AVOID IDLE THREATS LIKE THESE

WITH A TWO-YEAR-OLD: "I am so tired of stepping on your toys! I've had it! No more toys—ever! For as long as you live, you can never play with another toy!"

WITH A GRANDPARENT: "I am so tired of coming into the kitchen to find you feeding the baby ice cream or pickles just because you like to see his contorted facial expressions! You are *never* to feed my child *anything* for the rest of his life!"

AN OLDER CHILD

"*My* mother-in-law is like an annoying third child: 'When's dinner?' 'I'm hot.' 'Can I have a cookie?' 'I don't wanna walk that far.' She hates the baby gates that I have to use to keep the twins from falling down the stairs and from getting into my husband's office. She won't step over them like the rest of the adults do, and she claims that she can't open them. I could either let her helplessness drive me crazy or use it to my advantage. If the twins are asleep downstairs and I don't want her to wake them up to play, I can 'accidentally' gate her upstairs. Sometimes I hear 'Jaaaaaaaaane . . . ,' but if I wait a few minutes to answer, she gets discouraged and reads a book until I go up and let her out."

—JANE

OFFER
LIMITED CHOICES

WITH A TWO-YEAR-OLD: "You may choose peas or carrots as your vegetable. You may not choose jelly beans or party mints."

WITH A GRANDPARENT: "You may choose the striped outfit or the one with dogs on it. You may not dress the baby in the romper Auntie Jane knitted for me when I was a baby. It was ugly 30 years ago, and it's ugly and moth-eaten now."

TAKE AWAY
PRIVILEGES

WITH A TWO-YEAR-OLD: "I won't let you have another bagel if you try to 'play' it in the CD player as soon as I leave the room."

WITH A GRANDPARENT: "I won't let the baby watch TV with you anymore if you change the channel from *Teletubbies* to *Love Boat* reruns as soon as I leave the room."

THINK LONG-TERM

OR WHY YOU SHOULDN'T MOVE AND FAIL TO GIVE NANA AND PAPA YOUR FORWARDING ADDRESS

They will say "Who's there?" when your child says "Knock knock" for the 74th time.

They are the only baby-sitters you can be sure would rush into a burning building to save your child.

They will pretend to eat the Play-Doh pizza (and they will pretend it's delicious).

They always have time to sit on the porch swing with your child after dinner.

They will teach your children quaint expressions like "Don't you be a droopy drawers now" and "Don't just sit there like a bump on a log."

They will take an appropriately long time to find your son in hide-and-seek, even though he always hides behind the recliner.

They don't mind mud pies on the deck and frogs in the sink.

They will buy several rolls of ridiculously overpriced wrapping paper for the school fund-raiser.

They will always let your children sit on their laps, even in wet bathing suits.

They will teach your daughter to sing "How Much Is That Doggy in the Window?" because that was your favorite song when you were little.

They will heartily agree with you that your child is the smartest, sweetest, most beautiful child who ever lived.

HOW TO RECLAIM THE TV ROOM FROM YOUR FATHER-IN-LAW

GODPARENTS:
THE BACK-UPS

What do getting caught in an animal trap, floating on a board in shark-infested waters, and being audited by the IRS have in common?

They are all more fun than planning for your own death.

But once you have a baby, you've got to do it. You may not care who inherits your collection of plastic snow globes, but you care *very* much who inherits your perfect child or perfect children.

You and your husband will have to sit down and compare the relative merits and faults of all of your family members and close friends in an effort to determine who can be trusted to care for your child in the event of your death. In all likelihood, you will have to decide what set of faults will be least harmful to your precious offspring.

You may want to make a chart such as the one on the following pages.

YOUR POTENTIAL

NAME: **LYDIA**

RELATIONSHIP: Sister-in-law

BIGGEST POSITIVE: Thrifty and clever; finds multiple ways to use old paper towel rolls, empty egg cartons, and detergent bottles

BIGGEST NEGATIVE: Craft-obsessed

POTENTIAL CONSEQUENCES FOR CHILD: The kid will get beat up on the bus because instead of having an L. L. Bean backpack and a baseball cap, he has a macramé tote bag and a handmade felt beret.

NAME: **NORA**

RELATIONSHIP: Cousin

BIGGEST POSITIVE: A thoughtful listener

BIGGEST NEGATIVE: Has been in therapy since 10th grade

POTENTIAL CONSEQUENCES FOR CHILD: Will analyze everything child does. For example:

NORA: *"Why did you draw this picture of you and your friends from the knees up? Is it because you feel as if you can't move? You are stuck with this particular group of friends and aren't able to escape the accompanying peer pressure?"*

CHILD: *"Uh … I just don't know how to draw feet."*

NAME: **CAROLYN**

RELATIONSHIP: Best friend since first grade

BIGGEST POSITIVE: Happy-go-lucky; fun to be with

BIGGEST NEGATIVE: Seems to lose one of everything (earrings, shoes, gloves, etc.)

POTENTIAL CONSEQUENCES FOR CHILD: Shouldn't be a problem unless she is taking care of twins.

REPLACEMENTS, GOD FORBID

NAME: **ROGER**

RELATIONSHIP: Brother-in-law

BIGGEST POSITIVE: Reads everything, including appliance warranties

BIGGEST NEGATIVE: Overly attentive to the minutiae of life

POTENTIAL CONSEQUENCES FOR CHILD: He will know what the weather was like in Costa Rica on the day the child was born, but he will not know what school the child attends, who his best friend is, or where he disappears to every Wednesday night at 8:22 P.M.

NAME: **BRAD**

RELATIONSHIP: Brother

BIGGEST POSITIVE: Everyone's best buddy

BIGGEST NEGATIVE: Gives everything a weird nickname

POTENTIAL CONSEQUENCES FOR CHILD: The kid will go to school and be unable to communicate with anyone. For example:

LUNCH LADY: *"What would you like, young man?"*

CHILD: *"Neg on the spuds and the poodly-noods, but double up on the tooty fruity and the cow juice."*

NAME: **LOUISE**

RELATIONSHIP: Aunt

BIGGEST POSITIVE: Exceedingly generous and sweet

BIGGEST NEGATIVE: Eccentric gift giver

POTENTIAL CONSEQUENCES FOR CHILD: The poor thing will be a laughingstock when she is invited to a party and the birthday boy opens the gift she brought: a coal miner's helmet; three letter openers, each shaped like one of the Wise Men; and a secondhand pair of pants with a used tissue in the front pocket.

NEW MOM
SEEKS SAME

You look into his eyes. He returns your loving gaze. You smile. He grins back. You reach over and stroke his cheek and he nuzzles your hand.

"I love you," you whisper to him. "I love you, but it's not enough. I need more. I need someone who understands what I'm going through, someone

who can make me laugh, someone who will listen when I need to let it all out, someone who . . ."

You reach over and stick your finger down the front of his diaper . . . "Someone who doesn't soak through a clean outfit every hour and a half."

"Yes," you admit to him, "especially that."

No matter how fulfilled you are spending time with your baby, you crave adult companionship. You ache to spend time with someone who doesn't drool, someone who doesn't depend on you to suction out her nostrils, someone who doesn't consider fiddling with her toes a stimulating way to spend an afternoon.

Your former co-workers are trapped at work. Your husband is good for jiggling the baby while he checks the football scores, but he would never be able to tell you that if you leave the baby wrapped in a light blanket as you lower her into her little bathtub, she'll resent the dunking a lot less. Your mom lives 1,200 miles away. You need to find yourself another new mom.

HOW TO PICK UP
ANOTHER NEW MOM

It used to be a cinch back when Marion Cunningham was raising Richie and Joanie. Mothers-in-law lived upstairs, herds of aunties were just around the corner, and three gals across the street were also home with new babies. Today, we may not even know our next-door neighbors, our best friends work from 8 A.M. until 5:30 P.M., and we're probably relieved that our mother-in-law is neither upstairs nor within drop-in range.

So how do you find a soul mate? Or even just a casual companion for a Tuesday afternoon?

Finding and getting to know another new mom is a lot like trying to meet a nice, single guy. A lot of the same techniques apply. In many ways, though, it's better. There are loads of things you *won't* have to

Not likely...

If I buy her a bagel, too, maybe she'll let me cop a feel...

concern yourself with when you attempt to hook up with another mom:

• You don't have to worry about how many other new moms she's been with.

• She doesn't care whether or not you've shaved your legs recently, and vice versa.

• She probably won't show up at a restaurant wearing tube socks with sandals and a Hawaiian shirt. And if she does, so what?

• You don't care if hair loss runs in her family.

• She won't embarrass you by wearing a Speedo on the beach.

• She won't try to get into the shower with you.

• It doesn't hurt your feelings if she thinks another new mom is prettier than you.

• If she buys you a cup of coffee, you don't have to worry

that she's thinking she can get to second base with you.

• She probably will not refer to intimacy in terms of bases anyway.

• You completely avoid the whole "when-to-boink" dilemma.

THE BEST PICK-UP JOINTS

To find yourself a nice, available new mom, you want to hang out where new moms tend to gather. Just as with a potential boyfriend, you want to look for moms in places you really frequent, doing things you really like to do. (Remember that fling you had with Steve, who spent all of his free time playing with his miniature trains? It's like that.)

Here are some of the best places to pick up another new mom:

1. THE PLAY GROUP

This is the mommy equivalent of the singles' bar. Moms pretend to go so that their 10-week-olds can make friends (the way a guy in a bar pretends he's there for a drink), but the minute they connect with a few other mothers, they're outta there.

2. CLASSES FOR NEW PARENTS

By signing up for a parenting class or workshop, you are putting yourself in the midst of other new moms who are interested in the same topics as you are. The advantage here is that you can connect with people the way you did in high school: If you liked to sit in the back of the room and pass notes, you won't want to hook up with a Front-Row-Always-Wants-to-Answer-the-Question mom.

3. CLUBS

Whether you join Mothers of Twins or La Leche League, you've got a ready-made group of women with a common interest related to mothering. If your own interests are a little offbeat—

PICK-UP TIP NO. 1

Don't be your mother-in-law. Refrain from questioning another mom's judgment unless she is offering her kid a cigarette or letting her munch on a razor blade.

---

say, Mothers Who Like to Nurse Their Husbands in Addition to Their Babies— then you'll probably have to start your own group.

4. BABY-SITTING ROOM AT THE GYM

You already know that you both are trying to get some semblance of your old shape back. If you notice a mom who visits the gym at about the same time you do, you can ask her to join you for coffee and a bagel after you work out. You've seen her at her sweaty worst: She'll only look better on a date.

5. EXERCISE OR SWIM CLASS FOR BABIES AND MOMS

Everyone will pretend she's doing the class for her baby,

but you've got to know that those six-month-olds aren't exactly begging to be dunked in the YMCA pool twice a week in January and February. Moms signed up to meet other moms (and also to give themselves *something* to write down on the calendar in the Tuesday and Thursday squares).

6. CHILDREN'S SECTION OF THE PUBLIC LIBRARY

This lends itself to some great pick-up lines about favorite children's books or parenting books. Also, you may find that if you begin reading to your child, you'll attract other tiny listeners. And where toddlers wander, mothers will follow.

7. PLAYGROUND / PARK / MALL PLAY AREA

You'll be able to observe moms in action supervising their own children and reacting to other little ones. When you see someone you think you might like to get to know, put your baby in the swing or sandbox next to her baby.

8. PEDIATRICIAN'S OFFICE

Often pediatricians cluster the well-baby appointments together in an attempt to avoid too much interaction between infants and sick children. If so, put down the 1996 *Parents* magazine and flirt a little.

9. BABY FURNITURE STORE

You'll find that it's easy to start a conversation about strollers or high chairs in this no-pressure environment, and because they'll be spending big bucks, moms will not be in a rush and will be eager to chat.

PICK-UP TIP NO. 2

Memorize the names and phone numbers of top-notch baby-sitters. Watch the moms flock to you as you start spewing out that info.

PICK-UP TIP NO. 3

Ask the mom's permission before executing a baby pick up, nose wipe, or snack offer. Your baby is the one you came with; the others have their own mothers.

10. BOOK SIGNING / AUTHOR TALK FOR PARENTING OR BABY BOOK

You've got built-in pick-up lines if you are queued up to get a book signed ("What did you think of the chapter on weaning?") and you may even be temporarily baby-less, so you'll be able to have a relaxed discussion.

New Mom Faux Pas

No. 3

**BRAGGING ABOUT YOUR KID
BEFORE THERE'S REALLY ANYTHING
WORTH BRAGGING ABOUT**

THE WORST PICK-UP JOINTS

Some places seem as though they would be hot spots for picking up new moms, but are actually poor choices for a variety of reasons. You may get lucky and find yourself a date, but the odds are stacked against you. Here are some examples:

1. THE GROCERY AISLE WITH DIAPERS AND BABY FOOD

Though you're likely to bump into other at-home moms in the baby aisle if you shop during the day, you'll bump into other *harried* moms who are on a mission to fill their carts before nap-time meltdown. No one is in a lingering mood. If you do see a mom who piques your interest and you are worried that this may be your only chance to make a connection, there's no harm in a little bump with your cart to necessitate an "Oh, excuse me!" and possible further conversation.

PICK-UP TIP NO. 4

Be like Wal-Mart: Have lots of everything and be willing to share: diapers, wipes, juice, crackers. Nothing turns another mom on like the offer of a free zwieback.

2. THE LAUNDROMAT AT NIGHT

Or most places at night for that matter. Most moms are too tired to venture out at night, especially for something as dreary as doing laundry. The Laundromat in the wee hours is a haven for single professionals or dads pitching in on the homefront after work. Don't waste your time.

3. ANYPLACE DURING NAP TIME

During nap time, generally recognized as 1 to 3 P.M., you'll find most moms at home trying to catch up on sleep, laundry, or reading. This is usually a Do Not Disturb time period.

PICK-UP TRUE TALE

*H*elen connected with another new mom in the grocery store, even though neither had her kids with her. They were both standing in the check-out line and rocking back and forth without realizing it. When Helen noticed what she was doing, and then noticed that the woman behind her was doing the same thing, she asked, "How old's your baby?" And a new relationship began.

FLIRTING PROPS

Having a neat kid toy or baby gadget or two may spark conversations with other moms. Here are some good and bad ideas.

GOOD FLIRTING PROPS

Booties that actually stay on baby's feet

New-fangled European bottle with six holes that mimics the breast so closely it could even fool your husband

Baby sling or other intriguing baby-holding device

Funky hat that stays put and also does what a hat is supposed to do

Dainty (though durable) quilt to lay baby on

The latest thing for teething

Cool, non-competitive interactive, stimulating, natural wood toy from Hearthsong catalog

CD that both moms and babies can tolerate

BAD FLIRTING PROPS

Binky Bear, who belonged to Great Aunt Flossie. Family history to you, just a grimy animal to the rest of us

Huge, overstuffed diaper bag/steamer trunk that advertises your neurotic over-preparedness

Tiara

Labor/childbirth photos (or any photos of you in a train wreck or having your appendix out—all equally unappealing)

Steve Martin head gear

10 BEST PICK-UP LINES

You're in a great pick-up spot, and have spotted a desirable new mom. You decide to approach her and . . . what do you say? Here are some great opening lines (be sure to deliver them with a smile):

1. "My baby wants to meet your baby, but he's bashful."

2. "With a baby that beautiful, I'm sure you've already looked into baby modeling, right?"

3. "I'll bet there's a good story behind that _____."

4. "This seems like a great group of women. I'm glad I saw the notice on the bulletin board at the pediatrician's office. How did you find out about it?"

5. "I see you have the same book on baby care that I do. What did you think of the chapter on nap schedules?"

6. "You seem to be having some trouble with your stroller. May I help you with it?"

7. "I was just looking at baby seats the other day. Would you recommend the one you have?"

8. "I have extra teething biscuits. Would you like one?"

9. "I seem to have forgotten to pack my wipes. Would you happen to have an extra?"

10. "Did you hear that JCPenney is having a terrific sale on onesies?"

10 WORST PICK-UP LINES

(AND WHY YOU SHOULD AVOID THEM)

1. "Wow! She's huge! Are you sure she's only three weeks old?"

She's sure.

2. "Is the baby's hair naturally curly?"

As opposed to what— a perm?

3. "Big foreheads are on your husband's side, right?"

Moms don't notice big foreheads on their own babies. Ditto bulging eyes and bobo ears.

4. "There's no one else here I want to talk to."

Negative comments appeal only to negative people.

5. "So how much weight did you gain with him?"

. . . or you could ask about hemmorhoids, or varicose veins, or stretch marks.

6. "My last friend was a real loser."

Refer to #4.

PICK-UP TIP NO. 5

Take a photo of the baby whose mom you would like to get to know. Then ask for her address so you can send her the photo once it's developed. Refrain from driving by her house once you know where she lives: That makes you look desperate and may land you in the pokey.

7. *"What's a nice mom like you doing with a crabby baby like that?"*

Twelve percent of the moms who get this line will be amused by it. Eighty-eight percent will not. Play the odds.

8. *"What's your baby's sign?"*

Too '70s.

9. *"You're using* disposables? *Do you know that it takes 109 years for them to decompose in a landfill?"*

You are trying to make a friend, right?

10. *"Check out this weird diaper rash. Have you ever seen anything like it?"*

This line works about as well at Mom-and-Me-Storytime as it would in a singles bar.

PICK-UP TIP NO. 6

Remember that what you wear will determine who approaches you. Start with the standard "mom uniform" (practical and machine-washable) and add something that might spark a conversation: a sweatshirt with a logo or a colorful scarf. Don't wear anything "fussy" and avoid skimpy: Other moms don't want to be reminded of their own post-baby problem areas.

Now why isn't anybody talking to ME...?

Sandy hasn't figured out that her negative T-shirt message is a turn-off.

Past my PRIME and I never even had one

THE PLAY GROUP SCOOP

A play group is a network of moms and babies who meet regularly (usually weekly, often in the morning when babies are most alert and content) and take turns hosting the group. Your baby will enjoy seeing new faces and begin to learn how to relate to other adults and babies. (Shhhhh . . . we know it's really for you.)

It doesn't matter where you live, you will end up with essentially the same cast of characters in your version of *As the Play Group Turns* as in nearly every play group in America. And it's likely that the *only* thing you will have in common is a baby of approximately the same age.

PICK-UP TIP No. 7

Steal something. "Accidentally" pick up another mom's baby toy so that you will have to call her to return it. Or, if you're a gambler, leave something behind with your name on it and maybe another mom will call you. Or maybe the YMCA's somewhat unusual custodian will call, but that's a risk you'll have to be willing to take.

THE PARENTING-BY-THE-BOOK MOTHER

She's read everything from Bettelheim to Spock, and every sentence she utters contains a quotation. She delights in telling other mothers what they are doing wrong. (And she wants the rules of the play group to be in writing.)

THE OBLIVIOUS MOTHER

The mother of the child who is an absolute terror develops an interesting coping mechanism: oblivion. Her little monster will be hitting, biting, and hair-pulling a mere three feet from her, but it's as if she has blinders on—she sits there demurely, seeing nothing and therefore having to do nothing.

THE MOTHER WHO THINKS HER BABY IS 18

She must really hurt for companionship, because this mom talks to her baby as if he were a senior in high school. You just want to tell her, "Listen, your baby doesn't care what time it is, where you're going next, or how you're going to avoid the rush-hour traffic. He is six months old. He cares where his bottle is. That's it."

THE ANNOYINGLY PERFECT MOTHER

Part Mary Richards, part Carol Brady, she is always on time, brings homemade snacks for the entire group (including juice and napkins), has extra wipes, and has a baby who appears to be moving on the same track of perfection. She is so damn organized and cheerful you just want to slap her.

THE ANNOYINGLY IMPERFECT MOTHER

She shows up halfway through play group, hassled and harried, with nary a baby supply in tow. Most of the time, her baby has a runny nose and a weird hack. Because she has forgotten to bring any toys, she encourages him to suck on everyone else's. After she's passed around some lethal germs, she asks to borrow a diaper, wipes, and a bottle.

MOTHER EARTH

She wears clothes she made herself with wool from her own sheep and nurses the baby during the entire play group. She does not allow her child to interact with plastic, and brings a bag of rough, wooden "toys" that look like stuff she picked up from the front yard. She plans to have 10 children and home-school them all.

MARY, MOTHER OF JESUS

She is the mother who thinks that her child is *special*. She can't conceive that another mom might feel as strong a mother-child bond as she does. She believes that she loves her baby more than anyone else in North America loves hers and that her baby—and *her baby alone*—is destined for great things.

THE COMEDIENNE

Everything from her son's unfortunately placed birthmark to the plight of the Afghan people is a big, fat joke. She likes being center stage so much that sometimes she forgets she has a baby with her. The other mothers have to inform her when the poor kid has rolled into the next room.

THE ANXIOUS MOTHER

She believes she is woefully inept at mothering and needs constant reassurance that she is not doing permanent damage to her child. She believes that everyone, including Leona Helmsley, would make a better mother than she would.

BABY CLUES

Sometimes it's hard to size up another new mom quickly enough. You want to know if you are agreeing to spend the afternoon with the Oblivious Mother or the Mother Who Thinks Her Baby Is 18. Just look at the babies: A quick glance will tell you a great deal about the mother, *before* you become involved:

THE BABY

hair-do →
← pierced ears
frills & bows
frills & bows
big girl shoes

THE MOM

Spends Saturdays at the mall • Pierced her belly button • Always runs 20 minutes late • Misses Kathie Lee • Saving up to have her teeth bleached • Prefers the pictures that come with the frames • Met the baby's father at a roller rink

THE BABY

dog hairs • hand-knit cap • 100% cotton shirt • cloth diaper • hand-me-down pants (100% cotton) • sheepskin slippers

THE BABY

squeaky clean ears • 3 layers • extra bib underneath • extra pacifier • non-skid soles

THE MOM

Makes her own jam • Listens to Cat Stevens records • Has four dogs (they sleep with her) • Made herself a macramé hammock • Plans to nurse baby until he is four • Heats with wood • Chops wood herself • Saving up to go trekking in Nepal • Hangs laundry out to dry

THE MOM

Types up her grocery list • Sweeps her driveway • Files every instruction manual (alphabetically) • Puts aluminum foil in bottom of oven to catch drips • Records her weight daily on a chart • Knows how to set the timer on her VCR • Always feeds her cat at 11:15 A.M.

THE WEARING-TWO-HATS MOM

You've made the decision: you *are* going to return to work. On the downside, you may miss the first time the baby eats a bow-tie pasta, you won't be able to participate in the Mommy and Baby library storytime at 10 A.M. every Tuesday, and you'll live with the ever-present anxiety that the baby-sitter will come down with walking pneumonia on the day of your big presentation to the board of directors.

On the upside, you get to talk to big people every day and use big-people words like "budgetary items" and "consensus building." You get an actual lunch hour *and* a paycheck every two weeks with your very own name on it. And you have a wardrobe that is not limited to five pairs of blue sweatpants and a collection of T-shirts that remind you that you used to have the time and energy to Walk for the Wetlands, Hike for Hunger, and Trot for Tibet.

There will be many hectic and harried days when you identify with the hamster running in her squeaky wheel (minus her tendency to overproduce and then eat some of the babies). But even though you'll realize there's no such thing as having it *all* (not even remotely), you'll likely find a teetering balance that works for you.

LUNCH HOUR TO-DO LIST

1. Grocery shop for the week (see list on back)
2. Pick up dry cleaning
3. Work out at gym
4. Get hair cut
5. Mail package at P.O.
6. Get gas
7. Get car washed
8. Prescriptions filled at drugstore
9. Eat lunch in car on the way back to office

TIPS FOR THE WORKING MOM

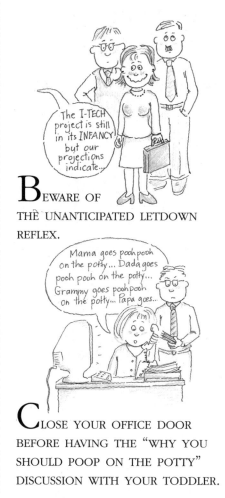

BEWARE OF THE UNANTICIPATED LETDOWN REFLEX.

CLOSE YOUR OFFICE DOOR BEFORE HAVING THE "WHY YOU SHOULD POOP ON THE POTTY" DISCUSSION WITH YOUR TODDLER.

IF YOU SNEAK OUT TO A GYMBOREE CLASS IN THE MIDDLE OF THE DAY, DON'T FORGET TO TAKE OFF YOUR NAME TAG.

CHECK THE CONTENTS OF YOUR BRIEFCASE *BEFORE* YOU GO INTO A BIG MEETING.

DAY-CARE OPTIONS
AND HOW BABY IS AFFECTED

	OPTION NO. 1	OPTION NO. 2
	NANNY MAJORING IN CHILD PSYCHOLOGY AT COLUMBIA	"AUNTIE" PEG'S HOUSE ACROSS THE STREET
DAY-CARE PROVIDER		
HOW IT AFFECTS WHAT IS GOING ON IN BABY'S BRAIN		
HOW IT AFFECTS THE WAY BABY WILL TURN OUT		

WHAT'S YOUR FAVORITE RADIO STATION?

QUESTIONS MOMS WISHED THEY HAD ASKED CAREGIVERS BEFORE THEY HIRED THEM

You know the kinds of questions you are supposed to ask prospective nannies or day-care providers: *What are your qualifications? Do you have references I can call? What are your thoughts on discipline? Sweets? TV? Do you smoke?*

But many moms say that although they are happy with their baby-sitters, there are questions that they never thought to ask during the interview process that they wished they *had* asked.

"*If I tell you that you need to put the dog on a leash to walk him, and my two-year-old tells you that the dog walks himself, so you can just let him out, who are you going to believe?*"

—KATHY

"*If* my son is in his I-am-a-dog phase, will you let him sample dog food?"

—KIM

"*Instead* of using the meat grinder I bought, are you going to chew the baby's meat yourself first before you feed it to her because that's the way they did it in the 'old country'?"

—MARY

"*Are* you going to fall in love with your karate instructor and spend all of the time you should be doing projects with my children looking through Bride's *magazine?*"

—KATE

"*Are* you going to decide that you want to leave an hour earlier than I get home and 'sub' your job out to another sitter for that hour?"

—DIANE

"*When* it's raining, are you going to call me at work and ask me to come home because you're afraid of thunder?"

—LISA

"*Are* you going to show the children how to dissect owl pellets at the kitchen table while *they are eating breakfast?*"

—MARY ANNE

"Will you believe me if I tell you that you can't put a metal pan in the microwave? Or will you have to prove it to yourself?"

—BETH

"Are you going to hide poopy diapers in wastebaskets all over the house that I won't discover until weeks later?"

—JULIA

"Will you call me out of a meeting to tell me that the baby's stuck in the cat door?"

—EILEEN

"If I have a big trip to the zoo planned with my son for Saturday—one that we've been talking about for two weeks—are you going to take him to the zoo the Friday before?"

—LIZ

"Do certain things go without saying? Feeding my son, for instance? Or do I have to specify that if I am gone for six hours that he will need to eat?"

—ERIN

"Will we be operating on the same concept of time? Like, when I say 8 A.M., what does that mean to you? Eightish? Or just sometime before nine?"

—CONNIE

WHY WOULD YOU DO ANYTHING TO KEEP YOUR BABY-SITTER?

Because she has a Ph.D. in your kid!

TRUE STORIES
EAU DE BRAZIL

"*At one time we had a nanny named Ana from Brazil who was quite exuberant and full of life. She would arrive in the morning with a bag of mini-Snickers bars that she'd distribute throughout the day. She would set up obstacle courses in the basement and take the kids to the park to throw water balloons. When I came home at night, she and the kids would be samba dancing. The kids had this amazingly fun-filled life with her that made my husband and me*  *look austere and rather dull. I couldn't possibly sustain Ana's level of excitement every evening and weekend.*

"With her hard-to-contain joie-de-vivre, life with Ana was going well—until she returned from a visit to Brazil with a gift for the kids: a huge bottle of what was essentially baby cologne or baby perfume. It looked like a two-liter bottle of Diet Coke. She began dousing the kids with it every day. But the smell was horrid, so intense that I almost couldn't stand to greet my own children when I got home from work. But I didn't want to hurt her feelings so I didn't say anything. Every night, though, I would dump a little of the stuff down the drain. Of course it took months for it to be all gone, but when it was, I celebrated!

"The next week she went back to Brazil for a visit and—you guessed it—returned with two bottles of the stuff!"

—LAUREN

ANXIOUS MOMENTS

HOW CAN BABY BE SAFE WITHOUT ME?

TRUE STORIES

EXPRESSING YOURSELF

Pumping Breast Milk While on the Job

"*I spend a lot of time in my car making sales calls. My day is so hectic that I often try to pump in the car. (I have a pump with a cigarette-lighter adaptor.) I know it sounds reckless, but I've actually gotten very adept at driving while pumping. One time my car swerved a little as I was making some pump adjustments and I looked up to see police lights flashing behind me! I pulled over and tried to get the breast pump off before the police officer came up to the window, but I failed. I was squirting all over the steering wheel when he asked for my license and registration.*"

—JEN

"*How's this for the ultimate cliché? Once I looked up when I was pumping in my office to see a window washer staring at me, or should I say at 'them.'*"

—ALYSSA

"*As I look back, I think I provided a little too much information to my co-workers. I used to put a 'Lactation in Progress' sign on my office door when I was pumping. 'Do not disturb' would have been sufficient.*"

—MARGE

"*I flew into Arkansas one day after having been delayed and rerouted. I absolutely had to pump, but there was no place for me to go and plug in my pump. I finally begged someone at one of the rental-car counters and she let me use an airport conference* room. The people who had been meeting in there wrapped up their business and left me alone."

—SUZANNE

"*I* had one of those dual Medela pump/corset kind of contraptions and was on my third day of pumping milk at work. I was talking on a conference call (distracted by the incessant whirring in the background) when I felt something wet on my lap. I had forgotten to screw on the bottles and I had been pumping the milk all over myself for a good ten minutes. I spent the rest of the day cloistered in my office trying to dry off for a big end-of-the-day meeting. That was the last day I pumped at work."

—CAROL

"*T*here is no outlet in our bathroom at work for my electric pump and I just didn't want to talk to my young, childless, male boss about why I needed one. So one Saturday my dad and I went into the office, found an outlet near the soda machines, and ran an extension cord through the ceiling tiles and then into the bathroom. No one ever commented on the dangling cord that mysteriously appeared in the bathroom."

—VICKI

"*I* found the walk from the bathroom to the kitchen holding the little bag of breast milk a very long one."

—RACHAEL

ADVICE FROM PEOPLE WITHOUT CHILDREN

"Of course you should go back to work! It'll be the best of both worlds!"

FIRST LAW OF
WORKING MOTHERS

You Cannot Avoid Getting
Baby Ickies on Your Clothes
No Matter How Long You
Wait to Get Dressed

6:16–6:22

6:23–6:26

6:27–6:35

6:36–6:49

6:50–6:54

6:55–7:00

7:05

- *Rice cereal with mashed bananas*
- *Baby boogies*
- *Milk stain with a crust (Life cereal)*
- *Hole in stockings from Matchbox backhoe*
- *Oops—pacifier is going to work, too*
- *Mismatched shoes, though both are black*

TRUE STORIES

WORKING MOMS DON'T MAKE QUICHE

S ome of the magazines aimed at working women would have you believe that other women are baking a month's worth of nutritious meals and freezing them, are ironing and laying out a week's worth of outfits every Sunday, and are working out at the gym by 5:30 every weekday morning, returning home in time to breast-feed before heading to the office.

Actually, there is only one woman who does this; they just keep writing articles about her. She is the same one who, in high school, was valedictorian, homecoming queen, captain of the tennis team, and president of student council, started a Foster Grandparents program, and dated a suave college guy.

For the rest of us, life is more about getting through the day. Working moms (anonymously) confess what their lives are *really* like:

"I haven't put baby photos in the album since she was three months old—she's almost two! I haven't filled in the baby book since she was about six weeks old!"

"I have been known to bribe my daughter with M&Ms to get her to go to the baby-sitter's."

"My mother-in-law likes to say, 'Don't try to make a happy baby happier.' I agree. So if he's happy in his baby swing, even if he's been swinging for 20 or 25 minutes, I leave him there."

"I refuse to buy anything for my daughter that requires 'some' assembly, no matter how badly she wants it."

"I bring our laundry to my mom's house and she does it for me."

"When we are on the run and the baby drops her pacifier, I just put it in my mouth to clean it off. By the time I'm on my third kid, I'll probably be letting the dog lick it off."

"I don't pay a lot of attention to warnings like 'Not intended for sleepwear.' If he falls asleep at 7:30 in his Spiderman costume, so be it."

"By the time I get to the mending and hand-washing piles, my son has outgrown all the outfits that have gathered there."

"Sometimes our 'quality family time' is zoning out in front of the Discovery Channel."

"I let my toddler pick out his own clothes for day care: They never match, and half the time he pulls stuff out of the hamper to wear, but it avoids getting-dressed battles."

"I'll let my kids squirt whipped cream onto anything on their dinner plate if it'll get them to eat it."

9:27 *Go to home office.*

9:41 *Check e-mail; forward funny penguin joke to friends at work.*

10:03 *Go to bathroom and see if pimple is getting bigger.*

10:45 *Try calling client; when line is busy, call Crate & Barrel and order wine glasses.*

11:17 *Answer nanny question.*

"Can I comb her hair?"

11:29 *Let cat in.*

11:41 *Try client again; leave a voice mail. Toy with idea of trying home perm kit.*

12:37 *Chat with nice lady calling to see if you need vinyl siding.*

12:48 *Let cat out.*

HOME: YOUR DAY

EPILOGUE

CONTEMPLATING THE FUTURE

Eventually your parenting job will be reduced to two basic activities:

"Here, Mom, hold this!" and "Mom, watch me!"

That's when you begin thinking about making baby number two. If you've always known you wanted four children (two boys, two girls, in that order), you won't have to pause too long before making that call. But if you are tallying up college costs or worried about the earth's population exploding, you may stop to ponder the pros and cons.

On the plus side, you get to use one more of your favorite names; you have another shot at passing along the elusive thick, black, curly-hair gene; and you'll get some extra mileage out of that ridiculously overpriced bassinet your first baby spent all of nineteen days sleeping in. You will provide your first with a live-in buddy (or sparring partner, but either way, they'll keep busy). And if you time it right, you'll be able to use the size XS pea-pod Halloween outfit again, too.

On the downside, you worry how a second child will affect the family dynamic: Will he or she throw off the fragile ecosystem that currently exists? And what about embarking on another pregnancy? You will have to endure nine more big, fat, nauseous months, though this time you'll have a better idea of what you're in for (and you won't confuse an errant piece of macaroni for your mucus plug).

It's a big decision. If you decide to go for it, refrain from sending a diaper as a baby announcement with the slogan: "We did Number Two!" (Yes, someone actually did that.)

And expect an all-new adventure. You may already know how to pat out a good burp and how to clean the baby's umbilical stump, but every baby is a surprise package.

Every baby is also a blessing. Enjoy!